Publish Your Book

Richard Lowe
The Writing King

Publish Your Book

Copyright © 2026 by Richard G Lowe

All rights reserved. No part of this publication may be reproduced, stored in a retrieval system, or transmitted by any means – electronic, mechanical, photographic (photocopying), recording, or otherwise – without prior permission in writing from the author.

Although every precaution has been taken to verify the accuracy of the information contained herein, the author and publisher assume no responsibility for any errors or omissions. No liability is assumed for damages that may result from the use of information contained within.

Trademarked names appear throughout this book. Rather than use a trademark symbol with every occurrence of a trademarked name, names are used in an editorial fashion, with no intention of infringement of the respective owner's trademark.

ISBN: 978-1-946458-24-7 (Paperback)

Table of Contents

See books by Richard Lowe at

https://masterofworlds.com

Get free publishing insights and industry updates at

https://thewritingking.substack.com

For ghostwriting and book coaching services see

https://thewritingking.com

Preface

Why have I written a book about self-publishing? Aren't there plenty of other books on the subject? Isn't the help within each platform sufficient?

My goal was to create a book that describes exactly, step-by-step, how to take a manuscript all the way through the process needed to publish on multiple platforms, without any diversions.

I've kept each platform simple and to-the-point and given notes on the various decisions you need to make throughout the process, and the ramifications of those decisions. By making the right choices at the beginning, you can make it easier later down the road.

The self-publishing landscape has changed dramatically since I wrote my first book on Kindle in 2016. What was once a simple choice between Amazon and maybe one other platform has exploded into dozens of options, each with its own requirements, benefits, and quirks. Authors today face the challenge of writing a book and then figuring out which platforms make sense for their goals and how to work with each one effectively.

I've broken this information into focused, practical guides. The first chapter covers the fundamentals that apply regardless of where you publish—manuscript preparation, cover design, metadata optimization, and the business basics every author needs to know. The remaining chapters dive deep into specific platforms, showing you exactly how to upload, optimize, and succeed on each one.

This approach serves multiple purposes.

If you're committed to Amazon KDP, you only need the fundamentals chapter and the KDP guide.

If you want to go wide with Draft2Digital, you can focus on those specific chapters.

If you're considering professional distribution through IngramSpark, you'll know exactly what's involved before you commit.

Each platform has its own personality, requirements, and optimization strategies. Amazon KDP now requires AI content disclosure and has updated royalty structures. Draft2Digital excels at wide distribution but requires different keyword strategies. IngramSpark opens bookstore doors but demands professional-grade files. Setup fees were dropped in 2023.

As of the writing of this book, I've published over one hundred volumes across multiple platforms, and I've learned quite a bit about how to make each platform work properly. The publishing world moves fast—AI tools have transformed content creation, royalty structures change, new platforms emerge, and old ones disappear. My purpose in writing this book is to pass along current, practical information that you can use immediately to get your books published properly and generating income.

The advice in this book comes from actual experience, not theory. I've made the mistakes so you don't have to. I've navigated platform changes, dealt with file upload failures, optimized for different algorithms, and learned which strategies get real results on sales versus which ones just waste time.

Most importantly, remember that the best publishing strategy is the one you'll execute. Don't get paralyzed by trying to master every platform at once. Start with the fundamentals, pick one platform, master it, and then expand from there. Your readers are waiting for your book—the key is getting it to them efficiently and professionally.

Introduction

I still remember the sick feeling in my stomach when I clicked "Publish" on my first book in 2016.

Three months of writing. Hundreds of hours of research. A cover I was proud of. And then... nothing. Zero sales for two weeks straight.

I'd fallen into the classic trap every new author falls into: I thought writing the book was the hard part. Wrong. The real challenge was figuring out how to get my book in front of people who wanted to read it.

Back then, self-publishing felt like throwing a message in a bottle into the ocean and hoping someone would find it. Amazon KDP was simpler but more mysterious. There were maybe five decent guides online, and most were written by people who'd published exactly one book and decided they were experts.

Today, I've published over one hundred titles across multiple platforms. I've made every possible mistake you can make in self-publishing, plus a few that seemed impossible until I stumbled into them. I've watched platforms change their rules overnight, seen algorithms shift without warning, and learned the hard way that what works today might not work tomorrow.

Authors are still making the same mistakes I made in 2016. They're still throwing their books into the void and wondering why nobody's buying them.

The Problem Nobody Talks About

Every self-publishing guide starts the same way: "Anyone can publish a book!" True. You can upload a Word document to Amazon KDP and have it for sale within 24 hours. Those guides conveniently skip the important part:

Anyone can publish a book, but most people publish it wrong.

They choose the wrong platforms for their goals. They price their books to fail. They write descriptions that make their books sound boring even when they're not. They pick categories where they have zero chance of being discovered. They upload covers that look amateur even when the content inside is professional.

And then they wonder why their book isn't selling.

I learned this the hard way when my second book also flopped spectacularly. Same problems, different title. I was missing something important about how this whole system worked.

The breakthrough came when I stopped thinking like a writer and started thinking like a reader. Instead of asking "How do I publish my book?" I asked "How do readers find and buy books online?"

Everything changed.

What This Book Actually Does

This isn't another "upload your manuscript and get rich" fantasy. I'm not going to tell you that self-publishing is easy money or that you'll replace your day job in six months.

What I will tell you is exactly how the major publishing platforms work, what they're looking for, and how to position your book so it has the best possible chance of finding its audience.

I'll also tell you about the mistakes I made so you don't have to make them yourself. Like the time I accidentally published the same book on two platforms and got kicked off one of them for violating exclusivity rules I didn't know existed. Or when I spent three days formatting a print book only to discover I'd used the wrong margins and had to start over.

You'll learn about the author who tripled his sales just by changing his book title. The romance writer who was languishing in obscurity until she switched to a different category and suddenly hit bestseller lists. The business book author who was pricing his book too low and leaving thousands of dollars on the table.

These aren't feel-good success stories. They're tactical examples of specific changes that produced measurable results.

The Real Publishing Landscape

The publishing world in 2025 looks like this:

Amazon still dominates, but their rules change constantly. What worked on KDP six months ago might get your account suspended today. They've cracked down on AI content, low-quality books, and anything that smells like mass-produced content. The easy money days are over.

Going "wide" with multiple platforms is more important than ever, but each platform has its own personality and requirements. Draft2Digital makes distribution simple but takes a cut of your earnings. IngramSpark opens bookstore doors but demands professional-grade files and charges revision fees after the first 60 days.

Traditional publishing is still very hard to break into, and even if you succeed, you'll wait years to see your book in print and give up most of your royalties for the privilege.

Hybrid publishers promise the best of both worlds but many are just expensive vanity presses in disguise.

Every option has trade-offs. Know what those trade-offs are before you commit your time, money, and manuscript to any particular path.

What You'll Actually Learn

Instead of generic advice that applies to nobody, you'll get specific strategies for specific situations:

If you want maximum income and don't mind being locked into Amazon's world, I'll show you exactly how to optimize for KDP Select and Kindle Unlimited.

If you want to reach the widest possible audience across multiple retailers, you'll learn how to set up distribution through Draft2Digital and why some books do better wide than exclusive.

If you're serious about getting into physical bookstores and libraries, you'll understand what IngramSpark requires and whether the investment makes sense for your goals.

If you're curious about traditional publishing, you'll learn what happens when you work with agents and publishers: both the benefits and the harsh realities they don't mention in the success stories.

You'll also learn how to avoid the landmines that blow up author careers. Like the seemingly innocent metadata choices that can get your book buried in Amazon's algorithm. Or the pricing strategies that signal "amateur" to potential readers. Or the cover design mistakes that cost you sales before anyone even reads your description.

The Truth About Publishing Success

After publishing over a hundred books, here's what I know for certain: there is no magic formula for publishing success. There are only better and worse decisions.

The authors who succeed long-term aren't necessarily the most talented writers. They're the ones who understand how the business side works and make strategic decisions based on their specific goals and circumstances.

They know when to go exclusive and when to go wide. They understand the difference between platforms that prioritize algorithms and platforms that prioritize human curation. They price their books strategically, not emotionally. They write descriptions that sell books, not just describe them.

They treat publishing as a business, not a hobby. That doesn't mean it can't be enjoyable or creatively fulfilling. But it does mean making decisions based on data rather than hopes.

This book will teach you to make better decisions. Not how to get lucky, but how to work with the system effectively.

Your book deserves to find its audience. Let's make sure it does.

The Simple Path: Publishing Your First Book

Everything in this book exists to help you make good decisions. But most authors do not need all of it for their first book. If you have a finished, edited manuscript and you want to get it published without reading ten chapters of platform comparisons first, this chapter is for you. It covers the path that works for most authors most of the time. Each step references the chapter where you can go deeper if you need to.

The Two Paths

Before the steps, a single decision: Do you want to publish on Amazon only, or do you want your book available everywhere?

Amazon only means using Kindle Direct Publishing for your ebook and print book. Your book will be on Amazon in most countries. It will not be in Apple Books, Kobo, Barnes and Noble, or available for libraries to order. This is the simplest setup. If you are not sure which path to take, start here.

Publishing everywhere, called going wide, means using KDP for Amazon and adding Draft2Digital for other ebook retailers and IngramSpark for print distribution to bookstores and libraries. It takes more setup time but gives your book broader reach. See Chapter 3 for Draft2Digital and Chapter 5 for IngramSpark.

This chapter walks through the Amazon-only path. Notes throughout indicate where the wide path diverges.

Step One: Get Your Accounts in Order

Go to kdp.amazon.com and create a KDP account. Use your legal name and real address. Complete the tax interview before you do anything else. Amazon holds royalties until it is done. Add your bank account for direct deposit. This takes about twenty minutes.

If you plan to go wide, also create accounts at draft2digital.com and ingramspark.com now, even if you do not use them immediately. See Chapter 2 for KDP account setup detail.

Step Two: Get an ISBN

For an ebook on KDP, you can skip the ISBN entirely. Amazon assigns an ASIN automatically and the book functions fine without an ISBN. Most authors publishing their first ebook on KDP only take this option.

For a print book, you need an ISBN. KDP will give you one for free. The catch: a A KDP-assigned ISBN lists KDP as the publisher in retail databases. If that does not bother you, use it. If you want your own imprint name as publisher, or if you plan to publish the same print book on IngramSpark. Buy your ISBN from Bowker at bowker.com. A single ISBN costs $125. A block of ten costs $295. See the FAQ, question 9, for the full ISBN explanation.

Step Three: Prepare Your Files

You need two files: your interior and your cover.

For an ebook interior: export your manuscript as a DOCX or EPUB from Word. KDP accepts both and converts DOCX automatically. For a simple text-heavy book, the DOCX conversion works fine. See Chapter 1 for what to clean up in your Word file before export, and Chapter 5 for how to prepare a proper EPUB if your book has complex formatting.

For a print interior: export your Word document as a PDF. Your page size in Word must match your trim size. If your book is 6 by 9 inches, your Word page must be 6 by 9 inches. See Chapter 5 for the full PDF export process.

For your cover: hire a designer who knows book covers in your genre, or use KDP's Cover Creator tool for a basic cover at no cost. Cover Creator produces acceptable results for authors testing the water. For a book you are serious about, hire a designer. Budget $200 to $500. See Chapter 1 for cover design fundamentals.

Step Four: Fill In Your Metadata

Metadata is everything Amazon uses to categorize and display your book: title, subtitle, author name, description, categories, and keywords. In KDP this happens on the Details tab during upload.

Title: exactly as it appears on your cover. No extra keywords stuffed into the title field.

Description: write it to sell the book, not to summarize it. Open with the reader's problem or the story's hook, not with what the book covers. See Chapter 1 for how to write a description that converts.

Categories: choose two from KDP's dropdown. Pick categories that genuinely match your book and where you have a realistic chance of ranking. You can request a third category by emailing KDP support after publication.

Keywords: seven slots. Use phrases readers actually type into Amazon search, not your own description of the book. "Small town cozy mystery with a cat" is a keyword. "Charming mystery fiction" is not.

Step Five: Set Your Price

For ebooks: price between $2.99 and $9.99 to qualify for KDP's 70% royalty rate. Most genre fiction prices between $2.99 and $5.99. Most nonfiction prices between $4.99 and $9.99.

See Chapter 2 for pricing strategy and the FAQ question 37 for ebook pricing guidance.

For print books: use KDP's royalty calculator on the Pricing tab to see your royalty at your chosen price after printing costs are deducted. Most trade paperbacks retail between $12.99 and $19.99. If your royalty at that price is less than $1.00 per sale, raise your price until it is. See FAQ question 38 for print pricing guidance.

Step Six: Publish

On the Content tab, upload your interior file and cover image. Use KDP's previewer to check every page. For ebooks: if it looks correct in the previewer, submit. For print books: do not approve distribution until you have ordered and reviewed a proof copy. Proof copies cost a few dollars plus shipping and are worth every cent.

Once you submit, KDP reviews your book. Ebooks typically go live within 24 to 48 hours. Print books take 72 hours or longer. You will receive an email when your book is live. See Chapter 2 for the full upload process tab by tab.

After You Publish

Go to authorcentral.amazon.com and claim your author page. Add your biography and photo. Connect all your books to your author profile. This is free and takes twenty minutes and it gets skipped. Do not skip it. See Chapter 2 for Author Central setup.

Check your KDP dashboard in a few days. If your book is not showing up in the categories you expected, contact KDP support and ask for specific category placement. If your print book looks wrong in the previewer, fix the file and resubmit before approving distribution.

The steps above get most books published correctly. Use the rest of this book when you need more:

Want your book in libraries and bookstores: Chapter 5 (IngramSpark) and Chapter 3 (Draft2Digital).

Want your book on Apple Books, Kobo, and Barnes and Noble: Chapter 3 (Draft2Digital) and Chapter 8 (Alternative Platforms).

Considering Kindle Unlimited: Chapter 2 (KDP Select decision).

Publishing an audiobook: Chapter 8 (Audiobooks section).

Considering a traditional publisher: Chapter 6.

Worried about publishing scams: Chapter 10.

Need more detail on any step above: the FAQ appendix has 139 questions with direct answers organized by topic.

Chapter 1: Self-Publishing Fundamentals

I've helped over 100 authors get their books published, and the same fundamental mistakes destroy promising books over and over again.

The patterns are predictable. New authors focus all their energy on writing, then treat publishing like an afterthought. They upload their manuscript with a cover made in PowerPoint, a description that reads like a grocery list, and wonder why nobody buys their book.

The difference between authors who succeed and those who fail isn't talent. It's understanding that publishing is where the real work begins. Your manuscript is just the raw material. The fundamentals covered in this chapter determine whether anyone will ever read it.

These aren't theoretical best practices. These are lessons learned from watching authors make expensive mistakes and then having to fix them later.

Professional Editing: The Non-Negotiable Investment

Professional editing isn't optional if you want to be taken seriously. A $600 copy editing investment can prevent career-ending disasters that destroy credibility and tank sales permanently.

Knowing which editor to hire saves you money and gets better results. Developmental editors restructure books that aren't working. They catch big-picture problems like confusing plot structure, weak character development, or disorganized content flow. Expect to pay $1,500-4,000.

Copy editors catch grammar and consistency issues that make authors look incompetent. They fix terminology problems, style inconsistencies, and basic readability issues. Budget $1,000-2,500.

Proofreaders are your final safety net. Even after professional copy editing, books still contain 3-5 errors that slip through. They catch typos, formatting errors, and minor mistakes for $200-500.

Authors who succeed understand that editing is an investment, not an expense. A cookbook author spent $900 on editing for her first book, which earned $15,000 in its first year. Her second cookbook, which she edited herself to save money, earned $400.

Can't afford professional editing? Then you need a systematic approach to self-editing. Read your manuscript aloud - your ear catches mistakes your eyes miss. Use tools like Grammarly or ProWritingAid. Get beta readers who aren't afraid to tell you the truth.

But understand what you're risking. Authors who skip professional editing to save $500 often lose $5,000 in potential sales.

Cover Design: Genre Expectations Trump Artistic Vision

Cover design isn't about creating art. It's about communicating to your target audience that your book is for them. Every genre has visual expectations, and violating them is expensive.

A romantic suspense author hired a professional designer and paid $400 for a beautiful cover. The problem? It looked like literary fiction. Clean typography, subtle imagery, sophisticated color palette. Perfect for Margaret Atwood, wrong for romantic suspense.

Romance readers expect different visual cues: passion, danger, attractive characters. Her cover said "serious literature" when her book delivered "escapist romance." After six months and $2,000 in advertising spend, she'd sold 47 copies.

Her relaunch with a genre-appropriate cover - shirtless man, bold typography, and the visual language romance readers expected - increased sales by 2,600% in the first month.

Thriller readers expect dark colors and bold fonts. Romance readers want passion and attractive people. Business book readers want clean, professional designs that suggest competence.

Study bestselling covers in your genre, then create something that fits those expectations while standing out slightly. A self-help author's first cover was bright yellow with cartoonish graphics that looked like a children's book. Self-help readers want covers that suggest transformation and success, not playground equipment. His relaunch with a professional, genre-appropriate cover tripled his sales in 30 days.

The technical specs matter too, but they're table stakes. Your cover needs to work at thumbnail size because that's how most people first see it. If they can't read your title when the cover is 100 pixels tall, they'll never click through to read your description.

Title Strategy: Searchability Beats Cleverness

"Maximizing Human Capital Through Strategic Leadership Development" was probably the worst title in publishing history. The author thought it sounded professional and academic. She was right - it sounded exactly like something nobody would ever search for on Amazon.

Her book about improving employee engagement sat at #2,847,392 in the Amazon rankings because no human being types "maximizing human capital" into a search bar. They search for "employee engagement," "leadership," or "team management."

Six months later, she republished the same book as "The Engaged Team: How to Build a Workplace People Love." Sales increased by 1,200%. The difference was keyword research. People search for "engaged team" and "workplace people love." They don't search for "strategic leadership development."

The common mistake is getting the process backwards. They write the book, then try to come up with a clever title. Smart authors research what people search for first, then build their title around those terms.

A marketing consultant tested this systematically. He published the same content under three different titles. "Advanced Methodologies for Customer Acquisition Optimization" sold 12 copies in three months. "The Customer Magnet: Proven Strategies for Business Growth" did better with 89 sales. But "Get More Customers: The 30-Day Business Growth Plan" crushed both with 267 sales in the same timeframe.

Same book. Same content. The only difference was how well the title matched what people searched for.

Subtitle strategy matters just as much. A romance author's book "Blood Moon" told readers nothing about what kind of romance it was. When she added the subtitle "A Paranormal Romance," sales doubled because readers could immediately identify the subgenre.

Book Descriptions That Sell

Technical accuracy doesn't sell books. Emotion does.

A management consultant learned this when his book description converted at 0.3%. One sale for every 333 people who read the description. His original description read like a textbook summary: "This complete guide covers seven proven methodologies for improving organizational productivity. Readers will learn systematic approaches to workflow optimization, resource allocation, and performance measurement."

Accurate? Yes. Compelling? Not even close.

The rewritten description started with a problem: "Your team is drowning in meetings that accomplish nothing. Projects take twice as long as they should. Good employees quit because they're frustrated with inefficient processes."

Then it promised a solution: "This book shows you how to eliminate the productivity killers that are costing you money and driving away talent."

The new description converted at 3.7%. Same book, same content. The difference was emotion instead of features.

Fiction descriptions need different approaches. Don't summarize your plot. Create intrigue. Start with conflict, introduce stakes, end with questions that make readers desperate to know what happens next.

One thing most authors miss: Amazon indexes your keywords and title for its own search. Google indexes your description as web content. These are two different systems with different rules. Stuffing your description with repeated keyword phrases might feel like optimization. it isn't. Google is built to penalize that kind of writing, and it will hurt your discoverability in search results outside Amazon without helping you inside it. Write your description for readers. Discoverability follows from writing that actually converts.

The fastest way to understand the difference between a description that informs and one that sells is to look at both side by side. Here's a bad one:

"This book is about self-publishing. It covers writing, publishing, and marketing your books on Amazon and other platforms. The author has many years of experience and shares his knowledge in this complete guide. Topics include book covers, metadata, social media, email lists, and more. Whether you are a beginner or have some experience, this book has something for everyone. Buy this book today."

Notice what's wrong. It leads with what the book is about instead of what the reader's problem is. "This book is about" is the weakest possible opening. "Has something for everyone" means it's for no one. The reader clicks away.

Here's the same book rewritten the right way:

"You wrote the book. So why isn't it selling? Most self-published authors sell fewer than a dozen copies, almost all to people they know. Not because the book is bad. Because nobody found it, nobody trusted it, and nobody clicked buy. That's a business problem, not a writing problem."

The rewritten version opens with the reader's frustration, not the author's credentials. It asks a question that stings if you're in that situation. The bad version describes a book. The good version talks to a person with a specific problem. That's the only difference that matters.

Keywords and Categories: Where Dreams Go to Die

Amazon gives you seven keyword slots with 50 characters each, and most authors waste them. They repeat words from their title, use obvious genre terms, or stuff them with synonyms nobody searches for.

One mystery author used "mystery novel detective crime thriller suspense" as one keyword. He thought he was covering all his bases. He was competing against every mystery book on Amazon for generic terms. Meanwhile, readers were searching for "small town detective" and "police procedural mystery."

Research what readers search for, not what you think they search for. Use tools like Publisher Rocket or KDP Rocket to find keywords with demand but manageable competition.

Categories determine who sees your book. Amazon's dropdown only shows major categories, not the subcategories where you want to compete. Getting into the right subcategory often requires emailing Amazon support or using special keywords.

Look at bestseller lists in potential categories. If every book has hundreds of reviews and you're starting with zero, pick a more narrow subcategory where you can rank.

One thing to know: Amazon now scans category placements and will remove your book from any category it decides isn't a genuine fit. The decision appears to be automated (likely an AI system) and there's no appeal process. You can wake up one morning with your book gone from a category where it was ranking, with no warning and no explanation.

The practical implication is to choose categories that genuinely match your book's content. Gaming the system with loosely related categories works until it doesn't, and when Amazon removes you, the ranking history goes with it.

Setting Up Your Publishing Business

You do not need an LLC or any formal business entity to publish a book. Thousands of successful indie authors operate as sole proprietors under their own names and have no legal or financial problems doing so. Publishing income gets reported on your tax return like any other self-employment income. Start simple and add structure when your revenue justifies it.

That said, there are reasons to consider a business entity as your publishing grows. An LLC separates your personal assets from your publishing business, which matters if you face a lawsuit over content in your books. It also makes it easier to open a dedicated business bank account, which simplifies tracking income and expenses for tax purposes. In most US states, forming an LLC costs $50 to $200 and takes a few hours.

A separate business bank account is worth doing even without an LLC. Mixing publishing income with personal finances creates accounting headaches and makes it harder to understand whether your publishing is actually profitable. Open a free business checking account when your first royalties arrive and route all publishing income and expenses through it from that point forward.

If you publish under an imprint name, register a DBA (Doing Business As) in your state before you buy your first ISBNs. The publisher name attached to an ISBN block cannot be changed after assignment. Your imprint name is what appears in retail databases and on library catalog records. Get it right before you buy.

Copyright: What You Already Have and What to Register

Your book is under copyright the moment you write it. You do not have to register it. You do not have to put a copyright notice on it. Copyright protection in the United States is automatic from the moment of creation.

That said, registration with the US Copyright Office matters for one specific reason: if someone infringes your copyright and you want to sue them for statutory damages and attorney fees, your work must be registered before the infringement occurs (or within three months of publication). Without registration, you can still sue for actual damages, but actual damages are hard to prove and often small. Statutory damages can be up to $150,000 per infringement for willful violations.

Registration costs $45 to $65 per work through the US Copyright Office at copyright.gov. You file online, upload a copy of your work, and receive a registration certificate in a few months. For most indie authors, registration is worth doing for books you expect to sell at scale or books that contain content someone might want to copy. nonfiction that gets widely shared, course material, and guides that could become templates.

Your copyright page should include: the copyright symbol, the year, and your name (or your publishing entity name). The standard line is: Copyright © 2025 by [Your Name]. All rights reserved. Add the reservation of rights language and any disclaimers specific to your genre. Nonfiction typically includes a disclaimer that the information is provided for educational purposes and the author assumes no liability for its use.

Interior Formatting Tools

Your Word document needs to be formatted for print before it becomes a book. Margins, fonts, paragraph spacing, headers, footers, page numbers, and chapter breaks all need to be set correctly for the trim size you are publishing in. You have three realistic options: format in Word, use dedicated book formatting software, or hire a formatter.

Word works and is what the majority of authors use. It handles everything a standard book needs if you know how to use it. The problems are the ones covered earlier in this chapter: styles must be applied correctly, section breaks must be set up properly, and the export settings must be right. Word is free if you already have it and produces professional results when used correctly.

Atticus is dedicated book formatting software designed for authors. It costs a one-time fee and runs in the browser. You paste in your manuscript, apply formatting using their templates, and export both print PDF and EPUB from the same file. The output is clean and professional. The limitation is that you are working within their template system and have less control over fine typographic details than you would in Word or InDesign.

Vellum is the premium option for Mac users. It produces some of the most beautiful ebook and print output available to indie authors and is widely used by professional formatters. It requires a Mac and costs more than Atticus. If you are on a PC, Vellum is not an option.

Hiring a formatter costs $50 to $300 for a simple book and is worth considering for your first book if you want to be certain the output is correct. A formatted book is easier to audit than a formatting process. Once you have one correctly formatted book as a reference, subsequent books are easier to format yourself.

Preparing Your Manuscript File for Upload

Before you upload anything to any platform, your manuscript file needs to be in the right state. Most upload failures and formatting disasters trace back to problems that existed in the Word document before a single file was exported. Fix these in the source file and everything downstream gets easier.

Start with a clean Word document. That means no tracked changes, no comments, and no hidden text. Go to the Review tab, accept all changes, delete all comments. Go to File, Options,

Display, and check Show Hidden Text to verify nothing is lurking. These elements embed in exports and can appear as visible markup in your published book.

Apply styles consistently throughout. Every chapter heading should use Heading 1 style, not bold text formatted to look like a heading. Every section heading should use Heading 2. Body text should use Normal. Consistent style application is what allows formatting software to recognize your document structure and what allows ebook converters to generate a working table of contents. A document where everything is styled as Normal with manual size and weight adjustments will produce an unusable ebook.

Use page breaks to start new chapters, not repeated Return presses. Go to the end of one chapter, insert a page break, and start the next chapter on the new page. Multiple blank lines between chapters look right on screen but produce irregular spacing in the final file. Insert, Break, Page Break in Word.

Remove double spaces after periods if your manuscript has them. Double spaces after periods are a typewriter convention. Published books use single spaces. Use Find and Replace: find two spaces, replace with one space. Run it until zero replacements are found.

Check your special characters. Em dashes, curly quotes, and ellipses need to be proper typographic characters, not hyphens standing in for dashes or straight quotes. Word usually handles this automatically if autocorrect is enabled. If your manuscript was written in another program or converted from another format, check that smart quotes and proper dashes are present throughout.

Set your page size to your intended trim size before you export anything for print. If you are publishing a 6 by 9 paperback, your Word document must be 6 by 9, not US Letter with margins creating a 6 by 9 text block. Go to Layout, Size, More Paper Sizes. Do this before you set your margins, because margins are calculated from the page edge.

For ebook export, your page size does not matter because ebooks are reflowable. But your heading styles, paragraph styles, and image placement do matter. Images should be inline with text, not floating. Text wrapping around images causes conversion failures. Tables should be simple. Footnotes may or may not convert cleanly depending on which platform you are targeting.

Save a master copy of your cleaned manuscript before you export anything. Call it something that indicates it is the source file: BookTitle_MASTER.docx. Every export for print or ebook comes from this file. If you need to make corrections, update the master file and re-export. Never edit the exported PDF or EPUB directly and never treat an export as your source of record.

The Publishing Checklist

Before you click publish on any platform, work through this list. It exists because the most expensive publishing mistakes are the ones discovered after the book is live.

Manuscript: professionally edited, proofread, and clean of tracked changes and comments. Styles applied consistently throughout. Page breaks used for chapter starts. Single spaces after periods. Smart quotes and proper typographic characters throughout.

Cover: genre-appropriate design by a professional or a well-researched DIY. Readable at 100 pixels wide. Correct dimensions for your trim size with full bleed. 300 DPI resolution. CMYK color mode. All text within the safe zone, away from the bleed edges.

Metadata: title, subtitle, and author name that match your cover exactly. Description written to sell, not to summarize. Categories that genuinely match your book. Keywords researched for actual reader search behavior. Publication date set correctly.

ISBN: purchased from Bowker, one for each format. Publisher name set to your imprint, not your personal name. Consistent across all platforms.

Interior PDF (for print): correct page size matching trim size. Correct margins with adequate gutter. Page numbers set up correctly with section breaks. Fonts embedded. Images at 300 DPI. Exported as Standard PDF, not PDF/A. Reviewed page by page before upload.

EPUB (for ebook): validated in Calibre or your conversion tool. Table of contents links work. Images display correctly. Chapter breaks land correctly. Opened in at least two reading apps before publishing.

Legal: copyright page complete with correct year and name. Disclaimer language appropriate to your genre. PCN or LCCN on copyright page if pursuing library distribution. All images used under proper commercial licenses.

Chapter 2: Amazon KDP

Amazon's Kindle Direct Publishing is the 800-pound gorilla of self-publishing. You can't ignore it. Amazon controls roughly 70% of the ebook market and a significant chunk of print book sales. Publishing anywhere else while ignoring KDP is like opening a restaurant and refusing to serve lunch.

KDP promises to make publishing easy: upload your book, set a price, and start selling within 24 hours. No upfront costs, no minimum orders, no warehouses full of books gathering dust in your garage.

Easy doesn't mean simple. KDP has more quirks than a sitcom character, and getting them wrong means your book disappears into Amazon's massive catalog like a tourist in Times Square. Brilliant books die in obscurity because their authors don't understand how the machine works.

Account Setup: Where the Real Work Starts

Setting up your KDP account seems simple until Amazon's verification process kicks in. One real estate author published under a pen name for two years when Amazon suddenly locked his account and demanded identity verification. His pen name didn't match his legal name, and he'd been using his business address instead of his home address.

Amazon's verification bot flagged the discrepancies and froze his account. His twelve books disappeared from sale overnight. His income dropped to zero. It took him six weeks to sort out the mess. Six weeks of lost sales, angry readers, and stress-induced insomnia.

Use your real name when setting up your KDP account. Amazon treats identity verification like a bank, not a bookstore. They cross-reference everything with government databases, and lying here gets your account terminated.

You can still publish under a pen name, but the account holder information must be accurate. Think of it as the difference between your stage name and your driver's license.

Tax information is equally critical. Amazon won't release any money until your tax status is verified. One romance author watched her book sell well for three months while her $500 royalty payment sat in Amazon's vault because she'd skipped the tax interview.

International authors face even more complexity with withholding rates and treaty benefits. One typo in your banking information can delay payments for months while banks try to figure out where to send the money.

The Publishing Process That Separates Winners from Losers

The upload process looks simple: manuscript, cover, metadata, publish. But each step has hidden traps that can kill your book's chances.

Title and subtitle get 200 characters combined, and authors consistently underestimate how important this is. One business author used 180 characters because he wanted to include every keyword he could think of. His final title looked like a desperate TV commercial.

Nobody could remember his title. Nobody could recommend it to friends. And it looked amateur.

Keep titles memorable and subtitles descriptive. "Digital Marketing Mastery: Proven Strategies for Small Business Growth" works better than keyword soup.

Series information causes its own headaches. One romance author published three books with slightly different series names: "Midnight Chronicles," "The Midnight Chronicles," and "Midnight Chronicles Series." Amazon treated these as three different series, so readers couldn't find all her books in one place.

The KDP Upload Process: Tab by Tab

The actual upload in KDP happens across three tabs: Details, Content, and Pricing. Each tab has decisions that affect your book permanently if you get them wrong.

The Details tab is where you enter your metadata. Start with your title, exactly as it appears on your cover, and your subtitle if you have one. If your book is part of a series, enter the series name and number here and use the same spelling every time across all books in that series. Leave the edition number blank for a first edition. Enter your author name as you want it to appear on the book page, and add any contributors such as an editor, illustrator, or translator.

The description field is what readers see on your Amazon product page. For publishing rights, select I own the copyright if you wrote the book. You get seven keyword slots and two categories from the dropdown, and you can request a third category by contacting KDP support after publication. If your book is for children, fill in the age and grade range fields. Finally, answer the AI content disclosure question honestly.

The Content tab is where you upload your files. For ebooks, upload your EPUB or DOCX file. KDP converts DOCX automatically, which works for simple books and fails for anything complex. Upload a properly built EPUB if your book has anything beyond basic text. Your cover image uploads separately on this tab and needs to be at least 2,560 by 1,600 pixels in JPEG or TIFF format. Use the KDP previewer after uploading and check every page before moving on.

For print books, upload your interior PDF and cover PDF separately. KDP flags file errors immediately. Fix them before proceeding, and do not approve a print book without ordering a proof copy first.

The Pricing tab is where you set your royalty rate and list price. For ebooks, choose 70% for prices between $2.99 and $9.99, and 35% for everything outside that range. Enter your price in the primary marketplace, then decide whether to let KDP set international prices automatically using exchange rates or set them manually. Manual pricing takes more time but gives you control over each market. The KDP Select enrollment checkbox is also on this tab. Read what you are agreeing to before you check it.

For print books, KDP calculates printing costs automatically from your uploaded file. Your royalty is the list price minus printing cost minus Amazon's percentage. Set a price that leaves a real royalty after those deductions. If the royalty shows as $0.00 or negative, the price is too low.

The AI Content Disclosure Reality

Amazon now requires disclosure of AI-generated content, and authors are still figuring out what this means. The disclosure doesn't appear publicly, but getting it wrong can result in account penalties.

AI-generated content means the AI created it, even if you edited it afterward. AI-assisted content means you wrote it and AI helped with grammar, suggestions, or improvements. One requires disclosure, the other doesn't.

If you use Grammarly to fix grammar, that's AI-assisted. If you use ChatGPT to write entire paragraphs that you then edit, that's AI-generated. When in doubt, disclose. Amazon's detection algorithms are getting more sophisticated, and lying about AI usage violates their terms of service.

KDP Select: The Exclusivity Decision

KDP Select is Amazon's exclusivity program. Enroll your ebook for 90 days of Amazon exclusivity, and you get access to promotional tools and Kindle Unlimited revenue.

The math gets complicated. One business author watched her Kindle Unlimited page reads generate $800 in the first month. She was thrilled until she calculated that those same page reads represented about 400 full book reads. At her $4.99 selling price, she would have earned $1,400 if those readers had bought the book instead.

But Kindle Unlimited readers might not have bought the book at full price anyway. They're subscription readers who prefer the all-you-can-read model.

Choose KDP Select if your genre performs well in Kindle Unlimited (romance, fantasy, thrillers), you're new to publishing and want maximum Amazon visibility, or you don't have distribution set up elsewhere yet.

One update from September 2025: Amazon changed KDP Select terms to allow enrolled authors to distribute their ebook to library platforms such as OverDrive and Hoopla without breaking exclusivity. Previously, KDP Select meant your ebook could not appear anywhere outside Amazon. Now you can be in Kindle Unlimited and still have your ebook in public libraries through a distributor like Draft2Digital, as long as you only enable library channels and not retail stores. If library distribution matters to you and KDP Select fits your genre, this changes the calculation.

Pre-Orders: When They Help and When They Don't

KDP allows you to set a pre-order date for ebooks up to 12 months before publication. Readers can purchase during the pre-order period and receive the book automatically on release day. Pre-orders for print books are not available on KDP. Print goes live when you approve it.

The case for pre-orders: they let you list your book on Amazon before it is finished, which gives you time to build advance reader interest. They also allow ACX to verify your Amazon listing exists, which is required before you can create an audiobook on their platform. If you are coordinating a simultaneous print, ebook, and audio launch, setting up the ebook pre-order first gives you the ASIN you need to start the ACX process.

The case against: Amazon assigns pre-order sales to the pre-order period, not launch day, which dilutes the ranking boost you would otherwise get from concentrated launch-day sales. If you miss your pre-order delivery deadline, Amazon penalizes your account and bans you from setting pre-orders for 12 months. Miss the deadline by uploading the wrong file and you have the same problem.

The practical guidance: use pre-orders when you have a finished or near-finished book and a specific launch date you are committed to, or when you need an ACX-compatible Amazon listing before your audio production is done. Skip pre-orders if you are not certain about your launch date or if you tend to revise manuscripts right up to publication.

Skip KDP Select if you want to publish wide across multiple platforms, your genre doesn't perform well in Kindle Unlimited (literary fiction, most nonfiction), or you have successful distribution elsewhere.

The promotional tools sound better than they work. Free book promotions can generate thousands of downloads, but free downloads don't improve your sales ranking. Countdown deals work better but are only available in the US and UK.

Pricing Strategy That Works

Amazon offers two royalty rates with different requirements and restrictions.

35% royalty is available for all prices and territories. Choose this if your book is priced under $2.99, has a large file size because of images, or you want maximum pricing flexibility.

70% royalty is available for books priced $2.99-$9.99 in most territories. Choose this for most ebooks. The higher rate usually outweighs any restrictions.

Print book royalties depend on your list price and printing costs. Amazon calculates printing costs based on page count, paper type, and ink usage. As of 2025, you earn 60% of list price minus printing costs for books priced at $9.99 and above. Books priced below $9.99 earn 50% minus printing costs.

Use Amazon's printing cost calculator to determine profitable pricing. Don't price print books so low that you make pennies per sale.

Low-Content Books: Journals, Workbooks, and Planners

Low-content books are print products with minimal text: lined journals, blank notebooks, planners, activity books, puzzle books, coloring books, and workbooks with fill-in templates. They are one of the most misunderstood categories in self-publishing because they look easy to produce and the market looks wide open. Both impressions are partly true and partly misleading.

KDP is the primary platform for low-content books and has specific rules for them. Books that are primarily blank pages, lines, or repeated templates must have a clear purpose stated in the title and description. "120 Page Lined Journal" is acceptable. "Blank Book" is not. KDP has removed large numbers of low-content books that lacked sufficient unique content or that duplicated existing listings. Do not upload the same interior with a different cover and call it a different book. This violates KDP's content guidelines.

Formatting low-content interiors differs from text books. You do not use first-line indents on blank or lined pages.

Page margins still matter, but the gutter consideration is more important because readers write in these books and need the inside margin wide enough that content is not obscured by the binding. A minimum of 0.75 inches on the gutter side is standard, with many designers using 0.875 or 1 inch for books intended for heavy use. Line spacing for ruled pages is typically 0.25 to 0.375 inches between lines.

The cover matters more for low-content books than for most other categories because there is no description or excerpt to sell the product. Buyers make their decision almost entirely on the cover design and the title. Genre and niche matter: a journal for grief recovery needs different visual language than a bullet journal for productivity enthusiasts. Study what sells in your specific niche rather than what looks good generally.

International pricing gets set automatically based on your US price, but you can adjust these manually. Consider local market conditions when setting prices.

Amazon Advertising: The Necessary Evil

Amazon advertising seems like the obvious solution until you see the costs. Competitive keywords can cost $1-3 per click, and most clicks don't convert to sales. Authors regularly spend more on advertising than they earn in royalties.

Start with Sponsored Product ads targeting keywords related to your book. Begin with a small daily budget ($5-10) and increase spending on keywords that convert.

Monitor your advertising cost versus royalty income. Profitable ads can run indefinitely and often improve organic rankings too.

Successful authors treat Amazon advertising like a loss leader. They're willing to break even or lose money on ads if those ads improve their organic ranking and long-term visibility.

The Optimization Game

Amazon's algorithm rewards books that sell well immediately after publication. This creates a cycle where successful books get more visibility, which generates more sales, which improves ranking, which generates even more sales.

New books start invisible to most shoppers. Your first 30 days are critical for Amazon's algorithm. Books that sell well initially get better long-term visibility.

Launch tactics: have your email list ready before publication, schedule social media promotion, contact book bloggers in advance, consider running Amazon ads immediately.

Don't publish and hope for the best. Amazon rewards books that gain early traction.

Category climbing is the art of moving up Amazon's bestseller lists. Your book needs sustained sales over several days to move up in rankings, but a single slow day can drop you back down.

Reviews impact both the algorithm and buyer behavior. Books with more reviews sell more books. Legitimate ways to get reviews: ask your email list, provide advance review copies to book bloggers, use services like NetGalley, include review requests in your book's back matter.

Never buy fake reviews or review swap with other authors. Amazon's detection systems catch these activities and penalize accounts.

Common Mistakes That Kill Books

Metadata mismatches are the silent killer. Your cover says one thing, your manuscript says another, and your KDP metadata says a third thing. Amazon's systems flag these inconsistencies and may reject your book.

Make sure your cover, manuscript, and KDP metadata match exactly. Amazon's automated systems are unforgiving of inconsistencies.

Copyright violations are becoming more common as authors use AI tools to generate content. Use only images you own or have proper licenses for. When in doubt, don't use it or get explicit permission.

Quality issues get caught in Amazon's increasingly sophisticated quality checks. Books with obvious editing problems, nonsensical content, or signs of mass production get flagged for review.

Amazon's definition of "quality" is subjective and constantly evolving, but poorly edited books consistently get caught in these sweeps.

Success Metrics That Matter

Track the right metrics to understand your book's performance and make informed decisions.

Units sold tells you volume but not profitability. Page reads from Kindle Unlimited add revenue at lower rates than direct sales. Geographic sales data shows where your books are popular but not why.

Category rankings matter more than overall Amazon rankings for most authors. Sustained top-100 rankings in any category indicate good performance. Overall rankings change hourly and are harder to interpret.

Review average and count both impact buyer behavior and Amazon's algorithm. Track both the average star rating and total number of reviews.

Amazon advertising metrics: click-through rate, conversion rate, and advertising cost of sales (ACoS). Aim for profitable ads or ads that improve organic ranking.

When Amazon KDP Makes Sense

Choose Amazon KDP if you want to reach the largest possible audience, need fast publication (books live within 24-48 hours), want to learn self-publishing without upfront costs, or you're writing fiction or nonfiction that performs well on Amazon.

Amazon KDP works for every genre and most author situations. Even if you publish elsewhere too, ignoring Amazon means ignoring 70% of the ebook market.

Skip Amazon as your only platform if you want to maximize long-term income through higher royalty rates elsewhere, you're targeting international markets where Amazon has less dominance, or your book requires specialized distribution channels.

The platform constantly evolves, usually without warning. Features appear and disappear. Policies change overnight. What worked last month might get your account suspended today.

Despite all its quirks and mysteries, Amazon KDP remains the most important platform for self-published authors. Master its requirements, understand its limitations, and work within its system. Fighting Amazon is like arguing with gravity.

Author Central: Your Public Author Profile

Author Central is Amazon's free author profile platform, separate from KDP. Go to authorcentral.amazon.com and claim your author page. It takes twenty minutes and it gets skipped. That is a mistake.

Your Author Central page lets you add a biography, photos, a blog feed, videos, and your Twitter feed directly to your Amazon author page. More importantly, it is where you connect all your books to a single author identity. Without Author Central, books published under slightly different name formats may appear as separate authors on Amazon. "Richard Lowe" and "Richard G. Lowe" and "R. Lowe" are three different people to Amazon's algorithm unless you merge them in Author Central.

Author Central also gives you access to sales rank history for your books, editorial reviews you can add to your book pages, and the ability to report listing errors that KDP's backend does not let you fix directly. If your book page has a wrong publication date, a missing cover, or a description that did not update after you edited it, Author Central customer service can often fix it faster than KDP support.

Set up Author Central before your first book goes live, not after. Build your author profile, write a real biography, and upload a professional photo. The author page is part of your book page from a reader's perspective. A blank author profile with no photo and no biography signals an amateur operation.

Managing Your KDP Bookshelf

The KDP Bookshelf is the dashboard where all your books live. Once you have more than a handful of titles, managing them systematically matters. A book that was published and forgotten is a book that will eventually cause problems: an outdated price, a broken series link, or a cover that no longer fits your brand.

Keep a spreadsheet alongside your KDP dashboard. Track each book's title, ASIN, ISBN, publication date, current price in each territory, royalty rate, and distribution settings. KDP does not make it easy to see all your settings at a glance across multiple titles. Your spreadsheet is the master record.

Review your entire catalog twice a year. Check that prices are still appropriate. Check that series links are correct. Check that descriptions have not become outdated. Check that your KDP Select enrollments are intentional. Books auto-renew into KDP Select unless you opt out before the renewal date.

KDP Select renewal is the one that catches authors off guard most often. You enroll for 90 days and the enrollment renews automatically at the end of each term. If you decided to go wide but forgot to opt out of KDP Select before renewal, you are locked in for another 90 days. Set a calendar reminder seven days before each enrollment period ends for any book you might want to take wide.

Content Review Flags and How to Avoid Them

Amazon reviews books both at submission and after publication. A content flag can pull your book from sale without warning while review is underway, sometimes for days or weeks. Most flags are triggered by automated systems, not human reviewers.

Common triggers: covers that contain nudity, titles or descriptions that contain prohibited keywords, content that appears AI-generated without disclosure, files with embedded malware or unusual metadata, books that closely resemble already-published titles (suspected plagiarism), and books from authors whose accounts have prior violations.

Avoid flags by keeping your metadata clean and accurate. Your title, subtitle, series name, and the text in your book should be consistent. Do not put keywords in your title that do not appear in your book. Do not use other authors' names in your metadata. Do not claim your book is a bestseller in the title or description. These all violate KDP's metadata guidelines and trigger review.

If your book is flagged, you receive an email explaining the reason. Fix the specific issue, resubmit, and expect a few days for review. If the flag reason is unclear or you believe it is a mistake, contact KDP support directly. Document every communication in writing. If your account itself is flagged rather than a single book, the resolution process is slower and less predictable.

Updating Your Book After Publication

You can update your book on KDP at any time. Interior files, cover files, description, categories, keywords, and price can all be changed after publication. Some updates take effect within hours; others take a day or two.

When you upload a new interior file, KDP notifies customers who previously purchased the book that an update is available. They can choose to download the updated version or keep the original. This is useful for correcting errors but be aware that readers who purchased the original will see the notification. If the correction is minor, that may not matter. If you are doing a major content revision, consider whether that changes the book enough that previous buyers feel misled.

Print book updates work differently. Uploaded new interior files replace the file on record for future print orders. Books already printed and in transit are not affected. If copies are sitting in Amazon's warehouse, those copies get sold before the new file takes effect for warehouse fulfillment. For significant changes, order a new proof copy after uploading the revision to confirm the updated file prints correctly.

Price changes take effect within a few hours on Amazon's main marketplaces and within a day or two on international marketplaces. If you are running a time-limited promotion, change the price the day before it starts rather than the morning of, to account for propagation delay.

Chapter 3: Draft2Digital

Going wide used to be torture. Upload to Amazon, then spend weeks creating accounts on a dozen platforms, each with its own stupid requirements, payment systems, and metadata formats. By the time you finished, you'd lost your launch momentum and your sanity.

Draft2Digital promises to fix this: upload once, distribute everywhere. For many authors, it delivers. But like every tool that seems magical, D2D has quirks that can screw you if you don't understand them.

The platform works best when you know what you're getting into. Mess up the setup and you'll watch your launch fizzle while you play whack-a-mole with platform rejections.

The Strategic Decision Framework

The question I get most from authors trying to decide between KDP Select and going wide is: which makes more money? Wrong question. The right question is which fits how you write and how you sell.

If you write romance, fantasy, or literary fiction, going wide usually makes sense. Those readers exist on every platform. Apple Books has a substantial romance readership. Kobo dominates in Canada. Tolino serves Germany. Your books can earn real income across all of them at the same time, and none of those platforms require you to give anything up to be there.

If you write business books, the math changes. Business readers find books on Amazon. They don't browse Apple Books for their next leadership title. They search Amazon, they buy from Amazon, and when their colleague asks for a recommendation they send an Amazon link. I've tested this with my own titles. Going wide with business content doesn't expand your audience. It fragments your sales data and dilutes your Amazon ranking without replacing the lost momentum.

Nonfiction that isn't specifically business: self-help, memoir, health, history, sits somewhere in between. Worth testing wide, but watch the numbers. If 85% of your sales stay on Amazon after six months wide, that's telling you something.

The other thing nobody tells you: switching strategies costs more than people think. Moving a KDP Select book wide means waiting out the 90-day enrollment period, then waiting for the other platforms to catch up. Moving a wide book into KDP Select means pulling it from everywhere else, which creates gaps in availability and kills whatever momentum you'd built on Apple or Kobo. Test wide with new releases while your existing books stay where they are. Don't reorganize your whole catalog based on a theory.

What You're Really Signing Up For

Draft2Digital simplifies the technical aspects of wide distribution but doesn't eliminate the strategic complexity. You're still dealing with multiple retailers, each with distinct audiences, promotional cycles, and revenue patterns.

As of May 2026, Draft2Digital charges a one-time $20 activation fee for new accounts. Existing accounts are not affected. D2D also introduced a $12 annual maintenance fee per account for accounts that earn less than $100 net in a rolling 12-month period. That is total earnings across all your books combined, not per book. If your books together earn more than $100 net per year, the maintenance fee does not apply.

Beyond those fees, setup is simple. Name, email, tax information, payment details, and you're ready to upload. This simplicity masks the downstream complexity that emerges when your book hits different retail platforms.

Each retailer maintains its own approval process, content guidelines, and quality standards. Apple Books might approve your book in 24 hours while Barnes & Noble takes two weeks to reject it for image quality issues. Kobo approves it but miscategorizes it as erotica instead of romance. These aren't D2D problems, they're retail reality.

Timeline management becomes critical. Upload at least two weeks before your planned launch date. Factor in time for rejections, file revisions, and the inevitable platform that decides your perfectly acceptable book violates their ever-changing content policies. Your marketing calendar needs buffer time built in.

International authors face additional complexity with currency conversion and tax implications. D2D consolidates payments from all retailers into a single monthly deposit, handling currency conversion at their rates. Your royalty report shows sales in dollars, euros, and pounds, but your bank deposit arrives as one amount in your local currency. This simplifies banking but complicates market analysis.

Tax implications vary by country and sales volume. Research your local requirements for international income reporting. Some countries require detailed breakdowns by source country, which means more spreadsheet work to track where your sales originated.

Two content restrictions worth knowing before you distribute through D2D.

First, Draft2Digital will not distribute certain categories of books. Self-publishing guides are one of them. D2D banned the category due to market oversaturation from AI-generated content. If your book falls into a restricted category and you submit it, D2D won't just reject it and move on. They will lock the title in your account so it can no longer be updated or used. You lose access to the file and the listing. Check D2D's current prohibited content list before uploading anything in a potentially sensitive category.

Second, Apple Books will reject any book distributed through D2D that contains URLs pointing to competing retail platforms. If your book includes links to Amazon, Barnes &

Noble, or other stores, even in the back matter. Apple will refuse it.

You have two options: strip the competing URLs from your manuscript before distributing through D2D, or simply uncheck Apple as a distribution channel in D2D and handle Apple separately if you want to be on that platform. For most authors with links in their back matter, unchecking Apple in D2D is the easier path.

Where D2D Sends Your Book

Draft2Digital connects you to Apple Books, Barnes & Noble, Kobo, OverDrive library systems, Scribd, Tolino European markets, and dozens of smaller retailers. Each platform represents a different reader base with distinct preferences and behaviors.

Apple Books readers tend to pay higher prices and prefer polished, professional content. The platform attracts readers who value design and user experience. Marketing on Apple focuses on editorial features and seasonal promotions instead of algorithmic optimization.

Barnes & Noble operates more like a traditional bookstore with human curation playing a larger role. Staff picks and featured placements drive significant sales, but getting noticed requires understanding their editorial calendar and submission processes.

Kobo dominates international markets, especially Canada and Europe. Their readers often seek alternatives to Amazon and may be more receptive to wide authors. Kobo also offers more promotional tools for wide authors, including self-serve advertising options.

Library distribution through OverDrive opens institutional sales that can provide steady income streams. Libraries buy differently than consumers, often purchasing multiple formats and keeping books available longer than retail sales cycles.

Smaller retailers collectively generate real sales volume. Platforms like Scribd, 24Symbols, and regional retailers in various countries might individually contribute small amounts, but together they can represent 10-20% of wide distribution income.

Platform approval timelines vary significantly. Apple Books usually processes books fastest, often within 24-48 hours. Kobo typically takes 3-7 days. Barnes & Noble can be unpredictable, sometimes approving immediately and sometimes taking weeks for unclear reasons.

Don't count on simultaneous availability across all platforms. Your launch strategy needs to accommodate staggered release dates. Some authors use this to their advantage, launching on fast-approving platforms first to generate early reviews and momentum.

Technical and Formatting Considerations

D2D converts your Word document to ebook formats automatically, which sounds great until you discover that "automatically" has limits.

For simple text, novels, narrative nonfiction, anything without complex , the conversion works well across all platforms. Clean Word file in, readable ebook out. If this describes your book, don't overthink the formatting question.

The problems start with anything more complicated. Tables break unpredictably. Text boxes disappear or reflow in ways that destroy your layout. Drop caps look fine on Apple and broken on Kobo. If your book relies on visual formatting to communicate: charts, sidebars, callout boxes, and technical diagrams. Test the converted files on every major platform before you launch. What you see in the D2D preview is not always what readers see on their devices.

Images are the other landmine. D2D compresses images, and the compression varies by platform. A photograph that looks sharp on Apple Books can appear muddy on Barnes & Noble. Keep your embedded images at 300 DPI, but check the actual output. If image quality matters for your book, consider uploading a pre-built EPUB instead of letting D2D convert from Word.

Print through D2D routes through IngramSpark's network, which has its own requirements covered in the IngramSpark chapter. Don't assume your ebook file works for print. It doesn't.

How D2D Formatting Works and Where It Fails

Draft2Digital's automated Word-to-EPUB conversion is convenient and good for simple prose. Understanding where it breaks down saves you from discovering problems after your book is live.

D2D strips most of your Word formatting and rebuilds it using its own style templates. Your chosen fonts, custom paragraph spacing, and indentation get replaced. D2D gives you a choice of its own themes with limited control within them. If your book design depends on specific typography, upload a pre-built EPUB instead.

Footnotes and endnotes convert inconsistently. In some output formats they become clickable links. In others they render as plain text at the end of the chapter or disappear entirely. Test footnote behavior on every platform before you publish. Nonfiction authors who rely on footnotes need to validate this carefully.

Scene breaks need specific handling. Three asterisks or a centered symbol on a line converts reliably. Blank lines alone do not survive conversion. Some platforms collapse them. Replace blank-line scene breaks with a visible separator before uploading to D2D.

Front matter causes consistent problems. Copyright pages, dedication pages, and title pages with centered text or manual spacing often come through garbled. D2D has a front matter template system. Use it rather than trying to replicate your own design.

Tables almost never convert cleanly. Simple two-column tables sometimes survive. Anything with merged cells, shading, or more than three columns will likely break. For books with data tables, convert the table to an image at 300 DPI and embed it. That survives conversion where the table markup does not.

The D2D preview shows what the EPUB looks like in one rendering environment. Apple Books, Kobo, and Kindle all render EPUB differently. Download the EPUB from D2D after publishing and open it in at least two different reading apps before you consider the file finished.

Metadata Strategy and Optimization

Your Amazon metadata won't translate perfectly to other platforms and you need to accept that upfront.

Amazon's categories are its own internal system. "Business > Small Business & Entrepreneurship" on Amazon might become "Economics" on Apple Books or "Entrepreneurship" on Kobo. D2D does its best to map categories across retailers, but you'll sometimes end up in a category that isn't quite right. Check where your book lands on each platform after it goes live.

Keywords are an Amazon-specific obsession. Apple Books doesn't work that way. Their algorithm prioritizes editorial curation and category fit over keyword matching. The seven keywords you agonized over for your Amazon listing matter much less on Apple. What matters there is being in the right category with a cover that fits the genre. Kobo falls somewhere in between.

Your book description will likely need a plain text version. HTML formatting that renders beautifully on Amazon: bold headers, line breaks, formatted lists. These can display as raw code on other platforms. Write a clean plain text version of your description and use that for D2D distribution. You'll sacrifice some formatting flexibility and gain consistent display across every retailer.

Series linking is worth the extra attention. Amazon connects series books automatically if you enter series information consistently. Other platforms vary. Set up your series information in D2D carefully and verify on each platform that your books are actually showing as connected. Readers discovering book two shouldn't have to hunt to find book one.

Pricing Strategy and Revenue Optimization

Here's something nobody tells you about going wide: you can charge more on Apple Books.

Apple readers pay premium prices without blinking. Romance and fantasy authors regularly price at $5.99 or $6.99 on Apple while keeping the same book at $4.99 on Amazon. The Apple audience is less price-sensitive and more loyal. I've seen authors increase revenue 15-20% just by adjusting their Apple pricing upward while leaving everything else alone.

Barnes & Noble is different. Their readers expect pricing that mirrors the print world. A $12.99 print book with a $3.99 ebook feels right to a B&N customer. A $9.99 print book with a $7.99 ebook feels wrong, even if the math is identical. Mirror the traditional relationship between print and digital and you'll do better.

International pricing is where authors leave money on the table without realizing it. D2D converts currencies automatically, which is convenient but not optimal. A $4.99 book in US dollars is expensive in India and cheap in Norway. Check what local bestsellers are priced at in your genre and adjust accordingly.

Running a sale on one platform while keeping regular prices everywhere else usually shifts sales rather than increases them. Readers who follow your newsletter find the discounted price and buy there. Everyone else keeps paying full price. Coordinated promotions across all platforms produce better results and require a lot more planning.

Marketing Strategy Across Platforms

Nobody warns you about this part. Going wide doesn't just mean more stores. It means more jobs.

With Amazon only, your marketing job is clear: run ads, build your email list, get reviews, chase keywords. With wide distribution, you're suddenly dealing with five different systems that don't talk to each other, each with its own promotional logic.

Apple Books doesn't have author advertising. You can't buy your way into visibility there. Editorial features drive sales, which means you need Apple to notice your book. The way to get noticed is to have great cover design, a clean category listing, and to apply for their promotional opportunities through their portal. Some authors get featured; most don't. It's more like pitching a magazine than running ads.

Kobo has a self-serve promotional program worth using. Their feature deals and price promotions work well for authors with established backlists. Barnes & Noble has a promotional program too, but getting into it is more work than it's worth for most indie authors.

Your email list becomes your most important marketing tool when you go wide because it's the one thing that works everywhere. Send readers to a universal book link and let them pick their store. The link usually defaults to Amazon, which is annoying, but the alternative is sending five separate emails with five separate links and watching half your list delete it.

Your Amazon reviews don't follow you. A book with 200 reviews on Amazon has zero reviews on Apple Books, zero on Kobo, zero on B&N. You're building social proof from scratch on every platform. That's the part that takes years, not weeks.

Analytics and Performance Tracking

D2D's dashboard shows you the big number: total sales across all platforms. This is at the same time useful and misleading.

I've watched authors get excited about their monthly sales figures while missing that 90% of the revenue was coming from one platform and everything else was basically noise. The consolidated view hides what's actually working.

Get in the habit of checking each retailer's native dashboard separately, not just D2D's summary. Apple's reporting updates on a different schedule than Kobo's, which updates differently than B&N's. None of them match D2D's numbers exactly due to timing differences and currency conversion. This is annoying and normal.

The number that matters most isn't overall sales. It's which platform is growing and which is shrinking. If your Apple sales double over six months while Amazon flatlines, that tells you something important about your audience and where to focus promotional energy.

Don't try to run ROI calculations on marketing campaigns when you're wide. It's nearly impossible to know if a Facebook ad drove sales to Amazon, Apple, or Kobo. You can track clicks but not conversions across multiple retailers. Accept that marketing attribution is fuzzy and focus on overall revenue trends instead.

International Market Development

This is where going wide pays off in ways that catch you by surprise.

Canada punches above its weight for romance and fantasy. Canadian readers actively seek out non-Amazon options, and Kobo is genuinely popular there in a way it isn't in the US. I've had books where Canadian sales through Kobo nearly matched US sales. Nobody told me to expect that. I just checked the reports one day and there it was.

Australia and New Zealand are similar. Strong bookstore cultures, good reading habits, and less Amazon dependence than the US market. These aren't huge numbers individually, but together they add up.

European markets through Tolino, the dominant ebook platform in Germany, Austria, and Switzerland, can produce real income if your book has universal appeal. Germany in particular is a substantial ebook market. Literary fiction, thrillers, and romance all translate well. Books that are very specifically American in their references don't do as well.

India is growing fast but price-sensitive. A $4.99 book is expensive there. Some authors set region-specific pricing for Indian customers through D2D's international pricing options. Whether that's worth the complexity depends on how much Indian traffic you're seeing.

The honest truth about international markets: you won't know which ones matter for you until you've been wide for six months and actually read your geographic sales breakdown. Most conventional wisdom about which countries buy which genres is based on other authors' experience, not yours. Check your own data.

Playing the Long Game

Here's the part that determines whether wide distribution works for you: patience.

Amazon KDP Select gives you immediate tools: free promotions, Countdown Deals, Kindle Unlimited page reads. You can launch a book and generate income in week one. Wide distribution doesn't work like that. Getting established across five platforms takes months, not days.

The payoff is that you stop being vulnerable to a single company's decisions.

Amazon has changed its royalty structure, its content policies, its algorithm, and its review policies multiple times since I started publishing in 2016. Every time they make a major change, authors who went all-in on KDP Select get hurt. Wide authors feel it too, but they don't get wiped out.

Your backlist is where wide distribution really pays off. A book you published three years ago is still earning small amounts from six platforms instead of dying quietly on Amazon. Those small amounts add up across dozens of titles. That's a publishing business, not a publishing experiment.

The authors I've watched build sustainable publishing incomes over five or more years are almost all wide. The ones who burned bright and disappeared were usually all-in on Amazon. That's not a coincidence.

Platform Risk: What D2D Does Not Tell You

Draft2Digital is convenient and widely used. It is also a platform with a documented pattern of account terminations that authors need to understand before they build their publishing operation around it.

D2D terminates accounts without prior warning. The most common stated reason is creating multiple accounts, which their terms of service prohibit. The problem is that D2D's fraud detection flags legitimate authors as multiple-account violators based on criteria they do not disclose.

Authors with a single account, legitimate books, and years of publishing history report waking up to find their account closed, their books delisted, and their emails going unanswered. This is not rare. It is a consistent pattern documented across Trustpilot, the Better Business Bureau, and author forums going back several years.

When D2D terminates an account, they withhold royalties. Their terms of service state that pending orders at termination are fulfilled under the original terms. D2D earns commission on those post-closure sales. You receive nothing. There is no formal appeals process. Authors who contest the termination by email report receiving no response, or a response that restates the terms of service without addressing the specific situation.

The Smashwords merger in 2022 appears to have made things worse. Authors report delayed sales reporting, poor reconciliation between D2D and the partner stores it distributes to, and KYC (Know Your Customer) verification failures introduced in late 2025 that resulted in account locks while authors waited weeks for identity verification to process.

None of this means you should not use D2D. It means you should use it the way you use any platform that could disappear on you without notice. Do not rely on it as your only distribution channel.

Set up direct accounts on Apple Books, Kobo, and Google Play so that if D2D terminates your account tomorrow, your books are still live on the three largest non-Amazon ebook retailers. Keep local copies of all your book files, cover files, and metadata. Check your D2D dashboard regularly and export any sales data you might need. Do not let royalties accumulate there for months before checking on them.

The practical lesson is the same one that applies to Gumroad, to KDP, and to every platform in this book: no single company should control your entire publishing operation. D2D is a tool. Use it. Just make sure your books exist somewhere else too.

Is Draft2Digital Right for You?

If you want a stable foundation for wide print distribution that does not carry these risks, IngramSpark is a different kind of operation entirely. Ingram Content Group has been distributing books since 1964 and supplies the majority of the world's major publishers. They are not running automated fraud sweeps that accidentally close legitimate author accounts. Their enforcement is slower and more human. For authors who want a distribution partner that is genuinely stable, IngramSpark is the safest route. Chapter 5 covers it in full.

D2D is the right tool if your genre has readers on multiple platforms and you have the patience to let those platforms build. It's the wrong tool if you need quick wins, write business content that lives on Amazon, or don't have bandwidth to track five different dashboards.

The most common mistake I see: authors move their entire existing catalog wide at once because they read that wide is better. Don't. Test wide with new releases while your established books stay where they are. If the new releases perform well wide after six months, start moving the catalog. If they don't, you haven't disrupted anything.

D2D makes going wide easier than it's ever been. That doesn't mean wide is right for everyone. Know your genre, know your readers, and make the decision based on where they actually buy, not where you wish they would.

Setting Up Wide Distribution: The Actual Steps

The concept of going wide is simple. The mechanics are worth knowing before you start so you do not set things up in an order that creates problems.

Step one: buy your own ISBN before you upload anywhere. A Bowker ISBN for each format, ebook, paperback, and hardcover, from bowker.com. The ISBN is what allows your book to exist as the same product across multiple platforms. Do not use a platform-assigned free ISBN for a book you plan to distribute wide. Platform ISBNs lock the publisher name to that platform and cannot be transferred.

Step two: set up your KDP account and upload the ebook and print book there first. Exclude KDP expanded distribution entirely. That is IngramSpark's territory and KDP's terms for it are worse. Do not enroll in KDP Select if you want to go wide. Wait for KDP to confirm your ISBN before proceeding.

Step three: create your Draft2Digital account and upload the same ebook file. D2D will ask which retailers you want to distribute to. Check all of them except Amazon. Amazon is handled directly through KDP. Check Apple Books, Kobo, Barnes and Noble, OverDrive, Scribd, Tolino, and any others. Allow two weeks for all platforms to go live before your launch date.

Step four: create your IngramSpark account and upload your print book files. This gives you distribution to libraries and physical bookstores. In IngramSpark, do not enable Amazon distribution. Your KDP listing handles Amazon. Enable distribution to all other channels. Set your wholesale discount to at least 40%, preferably 55% if you want bookstore consideration. Set returns to no unless you have specifically chosen to allow them.

Step five: upload your EPUB directly to Apple Books and Kobo if you want access to their promotional programs. D2D covers both platforms for sales, but direct accounts give you access to promotional opportunities that D2D-distributed books cannot get.

Step five: set up direct accounts on Apple Books, Kobo Writing Life, and Google Play Books. D2D distributes to all three and handles the sales. But direct accounts give you access to promotional programs that aggregator-distributed books cannot enter.

Apple Books direct: go to authors.apple.com and sign in with an Apple ID. You will need an EPUB file that passes Apple's EPUB validator (run it through the free EPUBCheck tool before uploading). Apple requires a US bank account or a bank account in a supported country for direct payment. Once live, you can apply for Apple's editorial featuring programs through the Books for Authors portal. D2D-distributed titles cannot apply for these programs directly.

Kobo Writing Life direct: go to kobowritinglife.com and create an account. Upload your EPUB and cover. Kobo pays 70% on books priced $2.99 and above. The main advantage of a direct account is access to Kobo's promotional programs: price promotions, Kobo Plus inclusion, and the ability to set your book to free temporarily without going through D2D support. Kobo does not require exclusivity and has no enrollment periods.

Google Play Books direct: go to play.google.com/books/publish and sign in with a Google account. Upload your EPUB or PDF. Google pays 70% royalties with no price floor.

The reason to go direct with Google is that D2D does not distribute to Google Play. It is one of the few major retailers where aggregator coverage is absent. If you are using D2D for wide distribution and skipping Google Play direct, your book is not on Google Play at all. Given that Google indexes Play Books listings in search results, that is a real gap.

The most common mistake in this sequence is uploading to IngramSpark and enabling Amazon distribution, which creates a second listing that competes with your KDP listing and often confuses Amazon's catalog. Keep Amazon and IngramSpark distribution separate from each other.

Chapter 4: Lulu Self-Publishing

Pick up an Amazon KDP print book and a Lulu print book in the same trim size. Hold them both. The difference is immediately obvious. Amazon's paper is thin enough that you can see text bleeding through from the other side on dense pages. Lulu's standard 60# offset paper feels like an actual book.

That difference sounds trivial until you're selling a cookbook, a photography collection, a technical manual, or anything else where readers are going to judge the product by how it feels in their hands before they've read a word. For those books, the quality gap between Lulu and Amazon KDP Print isn't a minor preference. It's the difference between a book that looks like it came from a real publisher and one that obviously didn't.

Lulu isn't the right tool for every project. If you're publishing fiction or basic nonfiction where the words are the product and the physical book is just a delivery mechanism, Amazon KDP Print is cheaper and faster and perfectly adequate. But if your book is a premium product competing with traditionally published titles in its category, Lulu's quality is the point.

When Lulu Is Worth It

Print quality determines whether Lulu fits your publishing strategy. If your book benefits from superior paper, binding, or printing quality, Lulu's higher costs often justify themselves through reader satisfaction and premium pricing opportunities.

Cookbooks, art books, photography collections, technical manuals, and specialty content where presentation matters perform well on Lulu. These books compete directly with traditional publishers, and readers expect professional quality that matches the price they're paying.

Bookstore distribution opens opportunities that other print-on-demand platforms can't provide. Lulu's extended distribution reaches physical bookstores and libraries through Ingram's network. This matters for authors targeting institutional sales or building credibility through retail presence.

Academic authors, business professionals, and specialty publishers often find Lulu's distribution worth the extra costs. Getting your book into university libraries or available for bookstore special orders provides legitimacy that pure online sales don't offer.

Skip Lulu if you're optimizing for lowest costs. Amazon KDP Print offers significantly lower printing expenses if quality differences don't matter for your project. Most fiction and basic non-fiction work fine with Amazon's quality levels.

Also skip Lulu if you're primarily publishing ebooks. Their ebook distribution works like Draft2Digital but with fewer platform options. Dedicated ebook platforms offer better tools and distribution for digital-first authors.

Print Quality That Justifies Premium Pricing

Lulu's print quality consistently beats Amazon KDP Print and most other print-on-demand services. Their standard paper is 60# white offset, significantly heavier than Amazon's thin paper. You can upgrade to 70# white paper for premium weight, cream-colored paper that's easier on eyes, or 50% recycled paper for environmental appeal.

Binding options set Lulu apart from competitors. Perfect binding provides standard paperback binding with square spine. Case binding offers hardcover with cloth or paper-covered boards. Coil binding uses plastic spiral binding that lies flat when open. Saddle stitching provides stapled binding for books under 92 pages.

Cover finishes include matte for a non-reflective professional look, gloss for shiny eye-catching appeal, or laminated covers for extra durability. Hardcovers can include dust jackets with different paper stocks and finishes.

Color printing quality on Lulu justifies premium pricing. CMYK color mode is required. RGB files get converted but may not match your intended colors. Get your color mode right initially to avoid reprinting delays and color mismatches.

The quality difference becomes apparent when readers handle your books. Lulu books feel substantial and professional, while Amazon's print-on-demand often feels obviously cheap. This perception affects reader satisfaction and willingness to recommend your work.

Distribution Tiers and Market Reach

Lulu offers three distribution levels with different reach and royalty structures.

Lulu Direct sells only through Lulu.com with highest royalty rates. You keep 80% of profit margin after printing costs with no distribution fees. Limited reach but maximum earnings per sale. Good for testing market demand or specialty books with niche audiences.

Global Distribution sends your book to Amazon, Barnes & Noble, and major retailers through Ingram's network. There is no flat one-time fee. instead, distribution costs are built into the royalty calculation, which reduces your per-sale earnings compared to direct sales. Takes 6-8 weeks to appear in retail channels.

Extended Distribution adds bookstore and library ordering through Ingram's full wholesale network. Same royalty structure as Global Distribution. Distribution costs reduce your margin, but this tier opens bookstore orderability, library system access, academic retailer placement, and the returns policy that most bookstores require.

Extended distribution pays for itself if you generate bookstore sales or library orders. These institutional buyers often purchase multiple copies and represent ongoing revenue streams that individual consumer sales don't provide.

Consider your target market when choosing distribution levels. Business books, academic titles, and specialty content benefit more from extended distribution than romance novels or typical fiction.

File Preparation and Technical Requirements

Lulu expects properly formatted PDF files with professional specifications. They don't accept Word documents like other platforms. You need minimum 300 DPI resolution, proper margins for your chosen trim size, and CMYK color mode for color books.

Download Lulu's templates for your trim size and binding option before formatting your manuscript. Their margin requirements differ from Amazon's, and what works on KDP creates text cutoff problems on Lulu.

Cover files require front cover, back cover, and spine in one PDF with high-resolution at 300 DPI minimum, correct dimensions including spine width, 0.125" bleed on all edges, and proper text safety margins.

Lulu's cover calculator determines exact dimensions based on your page count and paper type. Spine width varies with these factors. Use their calculator instead of guessing. Incorrect spine width creates white gaps that make books look amateurish.

The technical requirements reflect Lulu's focus on professional quality. They're not trying to make publishing accessible to everyone. They're targeting authors who understand print production or are willing to learn it.

Pricing Strategy and Cost Analysis

Lulu's pricing structure takes some math to work out. For distributed books, your royalty equals 60% of profit margin after printing costs and distribution fees.

Calculate carefully: retail price minus printing cost minus distribution fee equals profit margin. Your 60% royalty comes from that final number.

A 200-page paperback priced at $12.99 with $3.50 printing cost and $1.50 distribution fee leaves $7.99 profit margin. Your royalty at 60% equals $4.79 per book.

Printing costs depend on page count, trim size, paper type, and color usage. Black and white books with standard paper cost roughly $0.02 per page plus $0.50-$0.85 for cover and $1.20-$2.40 for binding. Color printing adds about $0.15 per color page.

Research comparable books in your category before setting prices. Lulu's superior quality often justifies premium pricing compared to obvious print-on-demand products. Traditional publishers charge $15-30 for similar quality books in most categories.

Factor printing costs into your pricing strategy early. Books with many pages need higher retail prices to generate reasonable royalties. Sometimes editing to reduce page count improves profit margins more than increasing sales volume.

Where Lulu Fits in Your Publishing Strategy

Lulu works best for authors who view their books as premium products competing with traditional publishers. If your book's value proposition depends on professional presentation, Lulu's quality advantages justify the higher costs.

Art books, photography collections, technical manuals, academic works, and specialty content where readers expect quality perform well on Lulu. These markets tolerate higher prices when quality meets expectations.

Business authors targeting corporate buyers often find Lulu's professional appearance important for credibility. A cheaply printed business book undermines the author's expertise claims, while professional quality reinforces authority.

Educational markets, including libraries and academic institutions, prefer quality that withstands repeated use. Lulu's superior binding and paper handle institutional use better than cheaper alternatives.

Bookstore placement through extended distribution provides credibility that online-only sales don't offer. Having your book available for special order in physical bookstores positions you alongside traditionally published authors.

Timeline and Launch Considerations

Lulu's approval and distribution process takes longer than Amazon's near-instant publishing. Books need 6-8 weeks to appear in retail channels after approval. Plan launch timing accordingly.

Different retailers update their catalogs at different speeds. Amazon shows new books within 2-3 weeks while others may take the full 6-8 weeks. Your marketing calendar needs to accommodate staggered availability.

The longer timeline allows for more thorough quality control. Lulu catches formatting and file issues that faster platforms might miss. This reduces the chance of publishing a book with technical problems.

Use the extended timeline for advance marketing. Build anticipation while your book works through distribution channels. Pre-launch buzz can generate day-one sales when your book finally appears in stores.

Performance Tracking and Metrics

The number Lulu authors usually obsess over is the wrong one. Gross sales volume tells you almost nothing when your margin per unit varies significantly by channel.

What actually matters: profit per sale by channel. A direct sale on Lulu.com at 80% margin is worth more than two Amazon sales at 60% margin after printing costs. Run the math on each channel separately and you'll quickly see where to focus your marketing energy.

Watch your extended distribution sales for the first six months with realistic expectations. Some authors see consistent library and bookstore orders almost immediately. Others wait a year and see nothing. If you're in month eight with no institutional sales and no bookstore orders, the $149 extended distribution fee didn't pay off for your particular book in your particular market. That's useful information.

The metric worth watching that authors often ignore: reader comments about the physical book. When reviewers mention that your book "feels substantial" or "looks like it came from a real publisher," that's Lulu's quality doing its job. Those comments turn into word-of-mouth recommendations that Amazon print-on-demand books rarely get.

Common Strategic Mistakes

The file preparation mistake isn't just common. It's almost universal for first-time Lulu authors. Everyone thinks their Word document will work fine. It won't. Download their template for your specific trim size and binding before you format a single page. Not after. Reformatting 200 pages of manuscript because your margins are wrong is the kind of experience that makes authors switch platforms out of spite.

The spine width calculation trips people up constantly. It changes based on page count and paper type, and if you get it wrong your cover won't fit. Use their calculator every time, even on your third or fourth Lulu book, because different paper weights produce different spine widths.

The pricing mistake that costs real money: authors set their price based on what they want to earn, not what the market will bear. Do the math first. Figure out what your printing cost and distribution fee will be, then determine what royalty you need, then check whether the resulting price is competitive in your category. If your 180-page paperback needs to be priced at $19.99 to make $4 per sale and comparable books sell for $14.99, you have a problem before you publish, not after.

The comparison mistake is treating Lulu as a cheaper-or-more-expensive version of Amazon KDP Print. It isn't. It's a different product for a different situation. If you're comparing per-unit printing costs, you're already thinking about it wrong.

Is Lulu Right for You?

Lulu fills a niche in self-publishing: high-quality print books with professional distribution. If your project demands superior print quality or bookstore placement, Lulu provides capabilities that other platforms can't match.

Higher costs make sense when print quality impacts your book's success or when you're targeting markets that value professional presentation. For specialty publishers, academic authors, and creators of premium content, Lulu often delivers better long-term results than cheaper alternatives.

The platform works best for authors who understand they're paying for quality and distribution reach, not just printing services. If your book competes with traditionally published titles, Lulu helps level the playing field.

Choose Lulu when quality and professional distribution matter more than rock-bottom costs. Your readers will notice the difference, and many are willing to pay for it. Skip it when cost optimization trumps quality considerations or when your content doesn't benefit from premium presentation.

The authors who get the most out of Lulu are the ones who go in knowing exactly what they need and why they can't get it cheaper elsewhere. If that description fits your book, Lulu will deliver. If it doesn't, Amazon KDP Print is right there and it's free.

Setting Up Your Lulu Account

Go to lulu.com and create a free account. Complete the tax information during setup. Unlike KDP, which holds royalties until you complete the tax interview separately, Lulu processes this at account creation so it does not delay your first publication.

Lulu assigns ISBNs that list you or your imprint as publisher, not Lulu. This is a real difference from KDP's free ISBN, which lists KDP as publisher in retail databases. If you have your own Bowker ISBNs, you can use those instead. For Lulu Direct store sales only, you can publish without an ISBN entirely.

The Lulu Upload Process

Lulu's upload interface is called the Project Wizard. You choose your binding type and trim size first, and the wizard walks you through required files from there. Unlike KDP, which accepts Word documents and converts them, Lulu requires properly formatted PDFs for all print projects. Your files need to be right before you start.

Before you format a single page, download Lulu's template for your exact trim size and binding type from their templates page. Templates are available as Word and InDesign files. Use them. Lulu's margin requirements differ from KDP's and IngramSpark's. A file that passes inspection on KDP may have margins that cut off text on Lulu. Formatting to the wrong template is the most common avoidable Lulu mistake.

The cover wizard is separate from the interior upload. Lulu offers a browser-based cover designer with templates as an alternative to uploading a custom PDF. For anything custom, use their cover calculator to get the exact spine width based on your page count and paper type, give that measurement to your designer, and upload the resulting PDF. The spine width changes with every paper and page count combination. Use the calculator every time.

After uploading, Lulu runs an automated file check. Problems are flagged immediately: margins too narrow, resolution too low, color mode incorrect, spine width mismatch. Fix everything before proceeding. Do not approve a project with flagged issues and assume they will not show up in print.

Ordering a Proof and Reviewing Quality

Order a physical proof copy before you approve distribution. This is not optional for a Lulu book. The quality difference between what looks correct on screen and what looks correct in print is real, and Lulu's quality is one of the main reasons you chose the platform. Verify it before it reaches readers.

When your proof arrives, check it methodically. Open it flat and look at the gutter. Text that disappears into the spine is a margin problem. Check the color pages against your screen version. Color shift between screen and print is normal; significant shift means your CMYK conversion needs adjustment. Check the cover for bleed errors. Check the binding by flexing the spine. A well-bound book springs back. A poorly bound one does not.

If the proof has problems, fix the files and order another proof. The cost of two proofs is less than the cost of distributing a flawed book to readers who paid premium prices for premium quality.

Lulu and Local Printing

One use case for Lulu that authors rarely consider: it can produce short runs for local distribution when international shipping makes POD impractical.

Authors outside North America, Europe, or Australia, the markets where IngramSpark and KDP have local print facilities, face freight costs that can eliminate any economic advantage of POD. In those situations, Lulu remains useful for ebook distribution while a local printer handles physical books.

The Pacific island situation my client faced is a version of a problem many authors in smaller markets encounter. Model your actual landed cost before committing to any POD platform. Landed cost is the unit printing price plus freight to your location. A local offset printer frequently wins at quantities as low as 200 copies once freight is included.

Lulu vs. IngramSpark: The Practical Comparison

Authors regularly ask whether to use Lulu or IngramSpark for premium print. They are not quite alternatives.

IngramSpark is a distribution platform that also does print. Its primary value is the Ingram catalog and the wholesale network connecting your book to 40,000 retailers and libraries. The print quality is good but not Lulu-level on standard stock. IngramSpark is where you go to be in bookstores.

Lulu is a print platform that also does distribution. Its primary value is print quality. The distribution through Global and Extended tiers routes through Ingram anyway, which means IngramSpark gives you the same distribution reach with more direct control over your terms.

For books that need premium print and bookstore presence, the practical answer is: use Lulu for print quality and Lulu Direct for direct sales, and set up IngramSpark separately for wholesale distribution. Two platforms, two ISBNs, and more management overhead, but Lulu's quality combined with IngramSpark's reach.

Chapter 5: IngramSpark Professional Publishing

IngramSpark is the gold standard for professional book distribution. If you want your books in actual bookstores and libraries, this is where you go. IngramSpark distributes to over 40,000 retailers and libraries worldwide through the largest book distribution network on the planet.

But IngramSpark isn't for everyone. They demand professional-quality files and have strict requirements that will reject your book if you mess up. This isn't Amazon KDP where you can upload a Word document and hope for the best. IngramSpark expects you to know what you're doing.

Founded by Ingram Content Group, the company that distributes most of the world's books, IngramSpark gives independent authors access to the same distribution network used by major publishers. Your book sits alongside titles from Random House and HarperCollins in the same catalogs and ordering systems.

No setup fees. You upload your book at no charge. Revisions are free for the first 60 days after publication. As of early 2026, IngramSpark dropped revision fees entirely. Revisions are now free regardless of when you make them. They also charge a 1.875% market access fee on each sale, but for most authors that's negligible.

Why Paper Choice Makes or Breaks Sales

Authors obsess over cover design and ignore paper choice completely. Backwards thinking that costs sales.

Paper weight affects how your book feels in readers' hands, directly impacting their perception of value. A cookbook printed on thin 50# paper feels cheap and flimsy. Readers subconsciously question whether the recipes are worth following. The same cookbook on 70# paper feels substantial and trustworthy. Bookstore buyers notice this immediately.

50# white offset is standard and works for most fiction. It keeps printing costs low while providing adequate quality. Choose this for novels, memoirs, and books where content matters more than physical presence.

55# white offset costs more but signals higher quality. Use this for nonfiction books where credibility matters. Business books, self-help, and how-to guides benefit from the extra weight. The slight cost increase often pays for itself through higher perceived value.

70# white offset is luxury territory. Coffee table books, art books, and premium editions justify this expense. The paper feels substantial enough that readers expect to pay more. Don't use this for genre fiction unless you're positioning as a premium product.

Natural/cream paper reduces eye strain for text-heavy books. Technical manuals, academic texts, and long-form nonfiction work well on cream stock. Fiction readers often prefer it for lengthy novels. The downside is higher printing costs and slightly reduced text contrast.

Your paper choice should match your pricing strategy. Cheap paper with premium pricing creates cognitive dissonance. Expensive paper with budget pricing destroys profit margins. Match the physical product to the price point you're targeting.

The Cover Lamination Decision That Affects Shelf Life

Lamination isn't about looks. It's about survival in the retail environment.

Matte lamination resists fingerprints and feels more sophisticated. Use matte for literary fiction, serious nonfiction, and books targeting educated audiences. Bookstore staff prefer matte because it doesn't show handling damage. Libraries choose matte covers because they age better under heavy use.

Gloss lamination makes colors pop and attracts attention. Romance novels, thrillers, and books competing for impulse purchases benefit from gloss. The shiny surface catches light and draws eyes from across the store. But gloss shows every fingerprint and scratch.

Soft-touch lamination costs more but feels luxurious. Premium nonfiction, high-end cookbooks, and books targeting affluent demographics justify the expense. Readers can't resist touching soft-touch covers, increasing pickup rates in bookstores.

Your genre expectations matter here. Romance readers expect gloss. Literary fiction readers expect matte. Business book buyers expect professional finishes that signal quality without flashiness.

Consider your distribution strategy too. Books sold primarily online can use any finish because customers can't touch them before buying. Books targeting physical retail need finishes that enhance tactile appeal and resist handling damage.

The Strategic Discount Decision

Trade discounts aren't just numbers. They're strategic tools that determine where your book gets placed and how retailers treat it.

40% discount is the minimum for retail consideration. Retailers make barely enough margin to justify shelf space. Your book gets minimal promotion and may not survive poor initial sales. Use 40% only if your content is so unique that retailers will stock it anyway.

45% discount is the sweet spot for most books. Retailers make reasonable profit while you maintain decent margins.

This discount level gets your book considered for face-out placement and staff recommendations. Most successful indie titles use 45%.

55% discount matches traditional publisher terms and opens premium placement opportunities. Bookstores treat your book like a major publisher release. You get consideration for promotional displays, staff picks, and high-traffic placement. The higher discount only makes sense if increased placement drives significantly more sales.

Calculate your break-even points before choosing discounts. A 55% discount book that sells twice as many copies can generate more total revenue than a 40% discount book with limited placement. But you need realistic sales projections, not wishful thinking.

Regional markets affect discount strategy too. Independent bookstores in literary markets often stock books regardless of discount if the content fits their audience. Chain stores and airport retailers focus heavily on margin and may ignore anything under 50%.

Returns Policy and Cash Flow Reality

Returnable status isn't optional if you want serious bookstore placement. But it creates cash flow challenges that destroy unprepared authors.

Returns happen 6-18 months after initial sales. Your quarterly royalty statement might show great sales, then get hit with massive returns the following year. Budget for this reality or get surprised by negative royalty statements.

Seasonal books face higher return rates. Christmas books get returned in January. Back-to-school titles get returned in October. Plan cash flow around these predictable patterns.

Genre affects return rates significantly. Romance and mystery novels have lower returns because readers consume them quickly. Literary fiction and nonfiction have higher returns because bookstores over-order based on initial buzz.

Non-returnable status cuts your bookstore placement by 80% but eliminates return risk. Use this for specialty titles with dedicated audiences who will request your book. Technical manuals, local interest books, and niche hobby titles can succeed non-returnable.

Consider your financial situation honestly. Returns can trigger negative royalty balances that take months to recover. New authors often can't absorb these cash flow swings. Start non-returnable and switch to returnable once you have financial cushion.

One critical setting to confirm before you hit publish: returns. Make sure the option to allow returns is set to NO, and check it again. If you accidentally enable returns, bookstores can send back unsold copies at any time. IngramSpark refunds them from your account balance and mails you the books, which often arrive in unusable condition.

The detail that catches authors off guard: if you enable returns and then change it to NO, the window stays open for six more months. Get it right the first time.

If you're targeting library sales, which is one of the main reasons to use IngramSpark. There's one more step most authors skip: get a PCN number from the Library of Congress before you publish.

PCN stands for Preassigned Control Number. It's free, and it's what the US library system uses to catalog books. Set up an account at loc.gov/publish/pcn, submit your book information at least a week before your publication date, and you'll receive a Library of Congress Control Number within a few days. That number goes on your copyright page and in your IngramSpark metadata.

You can't use a KDP-assigned ISBN for this. You need your own ISBN from Bowker. Bowker is the only ISBN issuing agency in the United States. A single ISBN costs $125. A block of ten costs $295, and a block of one hundred costs $575.

If you plan to publish more than one book, buy the ten-pack at the start. The per-ISBN cost drops from $125 to $29.50. If you've published under an imprint name, you're eligible. Libraries won't buy books that aren't in their catalog system. This is the step that gets you in.

Distribution Strategy Beyond Just Being Available

Getting listed doesn't mean getting stocked. IngramSpark makes your book orderable everywhere, but retailers choose what to carry.

Bookstore placement depends on perceived demand, not just availability. Stores stock books they expect to sell quickly. Your author platform, marketing efforts, and local connections matter more than distribution terms.

Libraries buy differently than bookstores. They prioritize patron requests, professional reviews, and collection development needs. A book that fails in bookstores might succeed in libraries if it fills educational or community needs.

Academic markets require different approaches than trade retail. University bookstores focus on course adoption potential. Academic libraries emphasize peer-reviewed credibility and subject expertise.

Regional distribution varies significantly. IngramSpark reaches everywhere, but local wholesalers and distributors affect placement. Strong regional connections often matter more than global availability.

Build relationships with retailers instead of hoping for automatic placement. Personal connections with bookstore buyers, librarians, and educators drive more sales than passive distribution.

When Distribution Timing Matters

IngramSpark distribution isn't instant like Amazon. Books take 6-8 weeks to appear in all retail databases and ordering systems. Plan your launch strategy around these delays.

Holiday sales require early setup. Christmas books need IngramSpark distribution by September to appear in holiday catalogs. Back-to-school titles need June distribution for fall placement.

Seasonal marketing campaigns must account for distribution lag. Your book might go viral on social media, but bookstores can't order it if it's not in their systems yet. Launch social campaigns after distribution is complete, not before.

Book awards and publicity events create ordering spikes that expose distribution gaps. Nothing kills momentum like excited readers who can't find your book in stores. Ensure complete distribution before seeking major publicity.

Review timing matters too. Professional reviews in trade publications influence retailer ordering decisions. Time your review submissions to land after distribution is active but before retailers finalize seasonal orders.

The Real ROI Calculation

IngramSpark success requires different math than Amazon publishing. Lower per-unit royalties can generate higher total revenue through increased placement and higher retail prices.

Premium paper and binding justify 20-30% higher retail prices compared to obvious print-on-demand books. Readers pay more for books that feel professionally published. The increased price often offsets higher production costs.

Bookstore placement generates marketing value beyond direct sales. Browsers discover your book organically. Staff recommendations create word-of-mouth marketing. Physical presence builds author credibility.

Library sales create long-term value through ongoing circulation. A library book might be read by dozens of people over several years. Each reader becomes a potential fan who buys your future books.

Professional credibility opens speaking opportunities, consulting gigs, and media appearances that generate income beyond book sales. Authors with IngramSpark distribution get taken more seriously by event organizers and media contacts.

Calculate total author income, not just book royalties. A book that breaks even on direct sales might generate thousands in speaking fees, consulting revenue, and credibility benefits.

Strategic Decision Framework

Choose IngramSpark when bookstore placement aligns with your marketing strategy and target audience. Literary fiction, serious nonfiction, and books with regional appeal benefit most from physical retail presence.

Skip IngramSpark if your audience buys primarily online or your marketing focuses on direct sales. Genre fiction, specialized nonfiction, and books with strong online platforms often perform better with higher-royalty platforms.

Consider your timeline and perfectionism level. IngramSpark rewards authors who get files right the first time and plan launches carefully. Impatient authors who want to publish immediately should stick with faster platforms.

Your business goals matter more than platform features. Authors building long-term publishing businesses benefit from IngramSpark's credibility and distribution reach. Authors focused on immediate income generation might prefer platforms with higher royalty rates.

Don't choose IngramSpark because it seems more "professional." Choose it because bookstore and library placement supports your marketing strategy and target audience. The platform should serve your goals, not define them.

Bleed, Margins, and Trim: What They Mean

Three terms that trip up first-time print authors: bleed, margin, and trim. Getting these wrong is the most common cause of IngramSpark file rejections.

The trim size is the finished size of your book after printing and cutting. A standard trade paperback is 6 by 9 inches. That is the size of the physical book a reader holds. Your interior PDF page dimensions must match your trim size exactly.

Bleed is the extra image or color area that extends beyond the trim line. When a printer cuts a stack of pages to the trim size, the cut is not always exactly on the line. It varies by a fraction of a millimeter. Bleed ensures that if the cut runs slightly outside the trim line, there is no white gap at the edge of the page.

IngramSpark requires 0.125 inch (one eighth inch) bleed on all four sides for any page that has color, images, or design elements running to the edge. For interior pages with only text and standard margins, bleed is not required.

Your cover file always requires bleed on all four sides. Design your cover at the trim size plus 0.125 inch on every side. A 6 by 9 cover file needs to be 6.25 by 9.25 inches before accounting for the spine and back cover. IngramSpark's cover template calculator gives you the exact dimensions based on your page count and paper choice.

Margins are the white space between the text block and the page edge. The inside margin, called the gutter, needs extra space because it gets partially hidden by the binding. A book that opens flat with text running into the gutter is unreadable.

IngramSpark's guidelines specify minimum margins for each trim size. Use them as your floor, not your target. Generous margins are easier to read and look more professional.

File Requirements and Professional Standards

IngramSpark demands print-ready PDF files that meet commercial printing standards. No Word documents, no hoping your margins work out, no amateur hour. You need 300 DPI images, CMYK color mode, proper bleeds, and exact trim sizes.

Cover files must include spine width calculations based on page count and paper weight. Get this wrong and your cover won't fit. Use their calculator or hire someone who knows what they're doing.

Interior files need proper margins, consistent fonts, and professional typesetting. Text that runs into gutters gets cut off. Images without proper resolution look like garbage. Inconsistent formatting screams amateur.

Proof copies are mandatory for first-time uploads. Order one, check everything, fix problems before approving distribution. Changes after approval cost $25 each and reset your distribution timeline.

Color accuracy matters for books with graphics, photos, or branded elements. CMYK color mode ensures printed colors match your intentions. RGB files get converted with unpredictable results.

Market Positioning and Competitive Strategy

IngramSpark positions your book as professionally published. Bookstore buyers and librarians can't tell the difference between your book and one from Random House. This credibility opens doors that other platforms can't.

Pricing flexibility lets you compete with traditional publishers while maintaining reasonable margins. Premium production quality justifies premium pricing that pure print-on-demand can't support.

Professional metadata distribution reaches industry databases that influence purchasing decisions. Your book appears in professional catalogs alongside traditionally published titles.

ISBN ownership through IngramSpark establishes you as the publisher of record. This matters for media coverage, award submissions, and professional recognition.

Global distribution reaches international markets through established wholesale channels. Your book becomes available to bookstores worldwide without separate international publishing deals.

Common Mistakes and How to Avoid Them

File preparation errors cause 90% of IngramSpark rejections. Use their templates, follow specifications exactly, and order proof copies before finalizing.

Unrealistic sales expectations lead to disappointment. IngramSpark enables bookstore placement but doesn't guarantee sales. Your marketing efforts determine actual performance.

Cash flow problems from returns catch new authors off guard. Budget for negative quarters and maintain financial reserves to handle return cycles.

Wrong discount levels limit placement opportunities or destroy profit margins. Research your genre's expectations and calculate break-even points before choosing.

Timing mistakes waste marketing momentum. Plan distribution lead times into your launch strategy instead of rushing to publish.

Ignoring professional standards undermines credibility benefits. If your book looks amateur despite IngramSpark distribution, you've wasted the platform's main advantage.

Success Metrics and Performance Tracking

Track different metrics for IngramSpark than other platforms. Direct sales matter less than placement breadth and professional recognition.

Monitor bookstore orders, library purchases, and special requests separately from online sales. These institutional buyers represent long-term value beyond immediate revenue.

Professional credibility benefits resist easy measurement but drive career advancement. Speaking opportunities, media coverage, and industry recognition often trace back to bookstore placement.

Return rates indicate market fit and pricing accuracy. High returns suggest pricing problems or audience mismatches. Low returns validate your positioning strategy.

Regional performance varies significantly based on local connections and market preferences. Focus marketing efforts where placement translates to actual sales.

IngramSpark succeeds when authors understand they're paying for access to professional distribution networks and credibility benefits that extend beyond direct book sales. Choose it strategically, execute professionally, and measure total career impact instead of just royalty statements.

IngramSpark as Your Publishing Foundation

Every platform in this book carries some degree of risk. KDP can terminate accounts. D2D has a documented pattern of closures with no warning and no appeals. Alternative platforms come and go. IngramSpark is different.

Ingram Content Group has distributed books since 1964. They supply the wholesale network that most of the world's major publishers depend on. They are not a startup, not an aggregator, and not a platform running automated enforcement sweeps that catch legitimate authors in the crossfire. They are a distribution infrastructure company with six decades of relationships with publishers, retailers, and libraries worldwide.

That does not mean IngramSpark is perfect. Their interface is slower and more demanding than KDP. Their file requirements are strict. Customer support can be slow. But the risk that matters most, the risk of waking up one morning to find your account closed and your books delisted with no explanation, is not a risk IngramSpark carries in the same way.

For authors who want a stable publishing foundation, IngramSpark is the safest route for print distribution and wide ebook reach. Use KDP for Amazon. Use D2D for wide ebook aggregation, with direct accounts on Apple, Kobo, and Google Play as a backup. Use IngramSpark for everything that matters most: your print books, your bookstore and library distribution, and your long-term publishing infrastructure. The platforms that treat you like a publisher rather than a user are the ones worth building on.

That said, IngramSpark is not without enforcement risk of its own. Their Catalog Integrity policy, in place since 2020, allows them to remove titles without notice for content that violates their guidelines: unauthorized summaries and workbooks, books that mimic popular titles, misleading content, and books created using AI or automated processes.

There is at least one documented case of their AI detection incorrectly flagging a legitimate book about AI as AI-generated.

The difference from D2D is that IngramSpark enforces at the title level, not the account level. They remove specific books that violate policy. They do not appear to close entire author accounts without warning and withhold all royalties. For a legitimate author publishing original work, the risk at IngramSpark is getting a specific title pulled for a content flag that can usually be appealed and resolved. That is a manageable problem. Losing your entire account with no recourse is not.

IngramSpark Book Builder: Two Paths

When you upload content to IngramSpark, Book Builder gives you two options. The first is the manual path: you supply a print-ready PDF for the interior and a separate print-ready PDF for the cover. IngramSpark uses those files as-is. The second is the automated path: you upload a Word document and IngramSpark formats it into a PDF for you. The automated path sounds easier. In most cases it is not.

The automated Word conversion handles simple manuscripts adequately. A novel with basic chapter headings and standard body text will come through readable. The moment your book has any complexity, custom styles, chapter title headers, images, tables, or section breaks controlling page numbers, the automated conversion introduces errors that are hard to spot in the preview and embarrassing in print. If you care how your book looks on the page, supply the PDF yourself.

Preparing Your Interior PDF from Word

Word's Save As PDF produces files IngramSpark accepts, but the settings matter and the Word file must be set up correctly first.

Set your page size in Word to match your trim size before anything else. If your book is 6 by 9 inches, your Word page size must be 6 by 9, not US Letter with margins that approximate 6 by 9. Go to Layout, Size, More Paper Sizes and enter exact dimensions. This is what IngramSpark receives and what gets printed.

Set your margins to leave enough room for the gutter, the inside margin that gets bound. For a 6 by 9 book under 300 pages, 0.75 inch gutter with 0.75 inch outside margins works. For longer books, increase the gutter. IngramSpark publishes margin guidelines in Book Builder help for your specific trim size and page count.

Set up page numbers correctly before exporting. Standard convention: title page and copyright page have no visible page numbers, front matter uses Roman numerals, and the body starts at page 1. Word handles this with section breaks and the Link to Previous header/footer setting. Get this right in Word and the PDF will be right.

When exporting, go to File, Save As, PDF. In the options dialog, make sure ISO 19005-1 compliant (PDF/A) is unchecked. PDF/A restrictions cause IngramSpark to reject the file. Choose Standard (publishing online and printing) rather than Minimum size. Open the exported PDF and read through every page before uploading. What you see is what gets printed.

Preparing Your EPUB with Calibre

IngramSpark distributes your ebook as an EPUB. You can supply your own or let Book Builder generate one from your Word file. Book Builder EPUB works for simple books. Calibre gives you more control for anything more complex.

The basic Calibre workflow: export your manuscript as a clean DOCX, add it to Calibre, fill in the metadata fields, and convert to EPUB. Calibre produces a valid EPUB that IngramSpark accepts.

Before converting, clean up your Word file. Accept or reject all tracked changes and delete all comments. Remove text boxes. Calibre cannot convert them and they vanish from the output. Remove decorative fonts that are not standard. Ebook readers substitute their own fonts and unusual choices render incorrectly. Make sure all images are embedded, not linked.

After converting, open the EPUB in Calibre's viewer and read through it. Check that chapter breaks land correctly, that table of contents links work, and that images display. IngramSpark validates EPUBs on upload and flags errors. Better to find them yourself than to get a rejection after you thought you were done.

Word File Gotchas Before You Export Anything

The Word file is where most production problems start. These are the issues that cause PDF rejections, Calibre failures, and books that look wrong after printing.

Tracked changes and comments left in the document export into your PDF and EPUB as visible markup. Go to the Review tab, accept all changes, delete all comments before you export. Do not skip this step.

Styles not applied consistently break EPUB table of contents generation. If chapter headings are formatted manually, made bold and large by hand, rather than using the Heading 1 style. Calibre will not recognize them as headings. Your EPUB table of contents will be empty or wrong. Every structural element should use a named Word style, not manual formatting.

Section breaks control page numbering and header/footer behavior. A missing section break means front matter page numbers bleed into the body or headers appear on pages where they should not. Next Page section break is what you want between major sections.

Fonts that are not embedded do not travel with the PDF reliably. Standard fonts like Georgia, Times New Roman, and Garamond are safe. Unusual downloaded fonts need to be embedded explicitly or IngramSpark substitutes something else.

Images linked rather than embedded disappear when the file moves to another machine. IngramSpark does not have access to your local file system. Make sure all images are embedded in the document, not linked to external files.

Automatic hyphenation should be on for print. It improves justified text. Turn it off before EPUB export. Ebook readers apply their own hyphenation and double-applying it creates errors.

Chapter 6: Traditional Publishing

Traditional publishing is where publishers pay you an advance and handle all the costs of editing, designing, printing, and distributing your book. Sounds great, right? The reality is brutal rejection rates, years of waiting, and giving up control of your work.

Less than 1% of submitted manuscripts get picked up by major publishers. Even if you're part of that 1%, you'll wait 18-24 months from contract signing to publication. Then you'll earn royalties only after your book earns back the advance, which doesn't happen for most traditionally published books.

But traditional publishing still offers benefits that self-publishing can't match: professional editing and design, bookstore placement, media attention, and industry credibility. If you land a contract with a major publisher, they'll spend $50,000-$100,000 marketing your book. That's more than most self-published authors will ever invest.

The question isn't whether traditional publishing is good or bad. It's whether you understand what you're signing up for and whether it fits your goals and timeline.

The Query Letter: Your First Gate

Every traditionally published book starts with a query letter. This is a one-page pitch sent to literary agents describing your book, your credentials, and why it belongs in the market. Agents use query letters to decide whether to request more material. Most never will.

A query letter has four parts. The first is the hook, one or two sentences that capture the book's premise and stakes. The second is the synopsis, a paragraph or two describing the story or argument, the main characters or subjects, and how it resolves.

Third comes the market information: comparable titles published in the last three to five years that share your book's audience, with a sentence explaining how yours differs. Last are your credentials, covering relevant experience, prior publications, platform size, and anything that establishes why you are the right person to write this book.

The query is not a place to explain how long you worked on the book, what your family thinks of it, or why you believe it will be a bestseller. Agents read hundreds of queries a week. They are looking for reasons to say no quickly. Give them only what they need to say yes.

Query fiction with a completed manuscript. Agents will not request an unfinished novel regardless of how good the premise sounds. Query nonfiction with a book proposal, which can be submitted before the book is written. The proposal demonstrates your argument, your platform, and your ability to deliver.

The Book Proposal for Nonfiction

A book proposal is the standard submission document for nonfiction pitched to traditional publishers. It is a sales document, not a sample of your writing style, though sample chapters are included. A professional proposal runs twenty to fifty pages and takes weeks to write well.

A standard proposal includes an overview of the book and its argument, a market analysis, a competitive title analysis of three to five comparable books, your author platform numbers (email list, social following, speaking history), a chapter-by-chapter outline, and two to three sample chapters.

Publishers buy nonfiction on proposal because the market research and platform matter as much as the writing. A weak proposal with a large platform sometimes gets bought. A brilliant proposal with no platform rarely does. Build your platform before you write the proposal, not after.

Small Presses and Independent Publishers

The traditional publishing landscape is not just the Big Five: Penguin Random House, HarperCollins, Simon and Schuster, Hachette, and Macmillan. Thousands of small and independent presses publish books every year, many without requiring agent representation.

Small presses offer real traditional publishing: the publisher pays for editing, design, printing, and distribution. You receive a royalty. Rights revert to you under defined conditions. The difference from the Big Five is smaller advances (often none at all), narrower distribution, and less marketing infrastructure.

For certain categories of books, small presses are the right call. Regional history, poetry, literary fiction, academic trade books, and highly specialized nonfiction often find better homes at independent presses than they would chasing Big Five interest. A regional press with strong relationships in their territory will often do more for a book that fits their list than a major publisher treating it as a low-priority title.

Small presses usually accept direct submissions without agent representation. Research presses that publish books similar to yours, read their submission guidelines carefully, and follow them exactly. Small press editors read their own slush pile and respond more personally than large publishers. A rejection from a small press often comes with useful feedback. A rejection from a Big Five agency rarely does.

The Economics Nobody Talks About

Publishers operate like venture capitalists. They invest heavily in a few books they expect to become hits, while most of their catalog loses money. This model explains everything about how they treat authors.

When a publisher offers you a $15,000 advance, they're not just giving you money. They're making a bet that your book will generate at least $150,000 in revenue. Your advance represents roughly 10% of their minimum revenue expectations. If your book sells less than that, you've cost them money.

This explains why publishers drop authors after one underperforming book. They're not being mean. They're protecting their investment capital for authors who consistently hit revenue targets. Your feelings don't matter when their quarterly numbers are due.

The math gets worse when you dig deeper. Publishers need to sell 25,000-50,000 copies of a hardcover to break even on their investment. Most books sell under 1,000 copies total. Publishers stay profitable by having a few massive hits subsidize dozens of failures.

Your job as an author isn't just writing a good book. It's writing a book that can sell 25,000+ copies within the first year. Publishers can't afford to nurture slow-building careers anymore.

Why Platform Beats Writing Quality

Publishers care about your platform more than your prose because platform predicts sales better than literary merit. A mediocre book by someone with 100,000 social media followers will outsell a brilliant book by an unknown author.

This creates a catch-22. You need a platform to get published, but you need to be published to build a platform. Smart authors solve this by building platforms around their expertise, not their writing aspirations.

A financial advisor who writes a money management book has built-in credibility and audience reach. A marketing consultant who writes about business growth can use existing client relationships. A parent who blogs about raising kids with special needs has an engaged community ready to buy their memoir.

Publishers aren't looking for writers who want to build platforms. They want platform-holders who happen to write books. The writing can be fixed with good editors. Platform takes years to develop and can't be manufactured.

Fiction authors face different platform expectations. Publishers want evidence that readers will seek out your work, not just stumble across it. This might mean contest wins, short story credits, or an active following in your genre.

The platform requirements vary by genre and publisher, but the principle remains constant: prove people want to read your work before asking publishers to invest in it.

The Agent Game and How to Play It

Agents act as gatekeepers to major publishers, but they're running businesses, not charities. Understanding their economics helps you approach them strategically.

A good agent handles 20-40 clients and needs each client to generate enough commission to justify the relationship. At 15% commission, they need you to earn at least $20,000 annually just to cover their overhead costs for your account. They're looking for authors who can sustain long-term careers, not one-book wonders.

This means agents prefer authors with multiple book ideas, strong platforms, and professional attitudes. They're investing time in your career development, not just your current manuscript.. Approach agents like business partners, not fairy godparents.

The query letter process frustrates authors because it seems arbitrary, but agents use queries to assess both your book and your professionalism. A poorly written query suggests you're not ready for professional publishing, regardless of your manuscript quality.

Successful queries demonstrate that you understand your market, know your competition, and can articulate your book's what makes your book stand out. Agents want authors who think like business partners, not artists waiting to be discovered.

Research agents like you're hiring employees. Look at their recent sales, client relationships, and communication styles. An agent who's perfect for literary fiction might be terrible for commercial thrillers. Match your needs to their strengths.

What Your Agent Does After You Sign With Them

Signing with an agent does not mean the hard part is over. It means the next hard part is starting. Your agent now has to sell your book to a publisher, which is a separate process from signing with the agent and can take anywhere from a few weeks to several years.

Your agent's first job is to prepare your submission package. They will likely ask for revisions before they submit anywhere. A good agent knows what acquiring editors want to see and will push you to strengthen the manuscript or proposal before it goes out. Listen to this feedback. Your agent's credibility with editors depends on submitting work that is ready.

The agent builds a submission list: a ranked selection of editors at publishing houses whose lists match your book. This is where the agent's relationships matter most. An agent who has sold books to an editor at Riverhead or Knopf gets their emails read. An agent without those relationships submits to the same slush pile as unagented authors, just with a return address that gets slightly more attention.

Submission strategy varies by agent and book. Some agents submit to twelve to twenty editors at the same time. Others go out in smaller rounds, targeting their best prospects first and using any feedback from those passes to refine the pitch before going wider. Ask your agent how they plan to submit and why.

A good agent will explain their strategy clearly. Vague answers about "reaching out to their contacts" are not a strategy.

When an editor expresses interest, the agent manages all communication. You do not contact editors directly. You do not discuss terms. Everything goes through your agent. If multiple editors want the book, the agent may run an auction where publishers submit competing offers by a deadline. Auctions are relatively rare but they do happen, and they are entirely the agent's domain to manage.

How Agents Negotiate Contracts

The offer from a publisher is not the final deal. It is the starting point for negotiation. Your agent's job is to improve every term that can be improved, not just the advance amount.

Advance negotiation is the most visible part but often not the most important. A higher advance sounds better but carries risk. A book that does not earn back a large advance can damage your relationship with the publisher and make it harder to get a second deal. An experienced agent weighs the advance offer against realistic sales projections and does not always push for the maximum.

Royalty rates, escalation clauses, territory rights, subsidiary rights splits, option clause terms, and rights reversion triggers are all negotiable and all affect your long-term earnings more than the advance in many cases. A book that earns out a modest advance and goes on to sell steadily for five years generates more total income than a book that receives a large advance it never earns back.

Your agent keeps 15% of everything the publisher pays you, permanently, for that book. This includes the advance, all royalty payments, and any subsidiary rights income the publisher controls. The agent's commission is deducted before you are paid. You never write your agent a check. The publisher sends payment to the agency, the agency takes their cut, and you receive the rest.

What Your Agent Does After the Book Sells

Many authors assume the agent's job ends when the contract is signed. It does not. Your agent is your representative for the life of that book and your advocate for your career as long as you work together.

During production, your agent handles communication breakdowns, contract compliance issues, and disputes about editorial direction. If your publisher misses a contractual deadline, your agent follows up. If the cover is unacceptable and your contract gives you consultation rights, your agent escalates the conversation. You should almost never contact your publisher directly about a problem. Go through your agent first.

Your agent tracks your royalty statements and flags discrepancies. Publishers make accounting errors. Some errors are accidental; some are not. An experienced agent knows what royalty statements should look like for your sales volume and territory and catches numbers that do not add up. Exercising audit rights is rare but the agent makes that call if needed.

Your agent also manages subsidiary rights that were retained by you rather than granted to the publisher. Translation rights, foreign language deals, film and television inquiries. These come through the agent and the agent negotiates them. A foreign translation deal for a nonfiction book can generate real income years after the original publication date. An agent with strong foreign rights contacts earns their commission many times over. These are deals you would never find on your own.

When your relationship with a publisher becomes difficult: a new editor who does not connect with your work, a marketing team that goes silent, a publisher who wants a different kind of book than you want to write. your agent manages that relationship. They are the professional distance between you and the institution that controls your book. Authors who bypass their agents and try to manage publisher relationships directly almost always make the situation worse.

The Submission Strategy That Works

The standard approach to submission is backwards. They write their book, then look for agents and publishers who might want it. Successful authors research the market first, then write books that fit identified opportunities.

Study publishers' recent releases in your genre. What themes, styles, and approaches are they buying? What gaps exist in their catalog that your book could fill? Publishers think in terms of catalog development, not individual book merit.

Timing matters enormously in traditional publishing. Publishers plan their catalogs 18-24 months in advance around seasonal themes, cultural trends, and competitive positioning. A book about cryptocurrency submitted during a crypto crash won't get consideration regardless of quality.

Follow industry publications like Publishers Weekly and The Bookseller to understand market trends and publisher priorities. Submit books that align with where the industry is heading, not where it's been.

The most successful submissions feel inevitable to publishers. Your book fills an obvious need in their catalog, targets a proven market, and rides current cultural momentum. Make it easy for them to say yes.

Contract Negotiations That Protect Your Future

Most authors focus on advance amounts and ignore contract terms that affect long-term earnings. This is backwards thinking that costs serious money.

Rights reversion clauses determine when you get your book back if sales decline. Standard contracts keep your book indefinitely as long as it sells a few copies annually. Negotiate clear sales thresholds that trigger rights reversion. Your book might have a second life with a different publisher or in self-publishing.

Territory restrictions affect international sales potential. Publishers often demand worldwide English rights but lack effective international distribution. Consider limiting territories to regions where they have strong sales networks.

Option clauses give publishers first rights to your next book, often at unfavorable terms. These clauses can trap you with publishers who don't promote your work effectively. Negotiate clear timeframes and evaluation criteria for option exercises.

Royalty escalation clauses increase your percentage after hitting sales milestones. A book that starts at 10% royalties might jump to 12.5% after 10,000 copies and 15% after 25,000 copies. These clauses reward success and align publisher incentives with your long-term interests.

Audit rights allow you to examine publisher financial records if you suspect underreported sales. Publishers resist these clauses, but they're essential protection against accounting errors or deliberate manipulation.

After You Sign: What Actually Happens

Authors who land a traditional deal are rarely prepared for what comes next. The contract signing feels like the finish line. It is the starting gun for a process that takes one to three years and involves losing control of nearly every decision about your book.

The advance payment rarely arrives in one check. Standard contracts split the advance into two, three, or four payments tied to milestones: on signing, on delivery and acceptance of the manuscript, on hardcover publication, and sometimes on paperback publication. If your advance is $30,000 split three ways, you receive $10,000 when you sign, $10,000 when the publisher accepts your final manuscript, and $10,000 on publication day. The gap between signing and publication is typically twelve to twenty-four months. Plan your finances accordingly.

"Delivery and acceptance" is a contract term that authors underestimate. Delivery means you submit the completed manuscript. Acceptance means the publisher agrees it meets the standards set out in the contract. Publishers can reject a delivered manuscript as not acceptable and demand revisions before releasing the second advance payment. This is uncommon but it happens, especially when an author's final manuscript departs significantly from what was proposed.

The Editorial Process After Signing

Your manuscript goes through multiple editorial rounds before it reaches a copyeditor. First comes the acquiring editor's notes, a document that may run ten to thirty pages identifying structural issues, missing sections, pacing problems, and content that does not work. This is the developmental edit phase, done by your editor at the publisher's expense. Expect it to take six to twelve weeks after you deliver the manuscript.

You revise based on those notes and resubmit. The editor reviews your revision and either accepts it or sends another round of notes. Most books go through two to three editorial rounds before the editor is satisfied. The total time from manuscript delivery to editorial acceptance typically runs three to six months.

After editorial acceptance, the manuscript goes to a copyeditor who works on a schedule set by the publisher. You review the copyedited manuscript and respond to queries. The manuscript then goes to a proofreader. You review page proofs, the formatted text as it will appear in print. This is your last opportunity to catch errors. Changes at page proof stage beyond minor corrections are expensive and publishers discourage them.

Throughout this process, communication with your editor is professional but limited. Your editor has dozens of books in production at the same time. Response times of days or weeks on routine questions are normal. Editors who go silent for months are not unusual. Build your own timeline tracker and follow up professionally when milestones pass.

Cover and Design Decisions

You will almost certainly not have final say over your cover. Most traditional publishing contracts grant the publisher final approval over all design decisions. You may be consulted, and good publishers do consult authors, but consultation is not approval.

Publishers make cover decisions based on sales data, retail feedback, and what their art department believes will work in their sales channels. These decisions are sometimes wrong, and authors who were right have no recourse. You can express strong preferences, provide inspiration images, and escalate concerns to your editor. You cannot veto a cover you hate unless your contract specifically grants that right, which most contracts do not.

Interior design, font selection, chapter layout, and typesetting are entirely the publisher's domain. You will not be asked. You will receive page proofs after these decisions are made and your role is to check for errors, not to redesign the layout.

Catalog placement determines how the publisher positions and promotes your book before it is published. A lead title gets front catalog placement, advance reading copies distributed widely, and the sales team's active attention when calling on accounts. A mid-list title gets standard catalog listing and minimal sales focus.

You find out where you land when the catalog is published, usually six to nine months before your book releases. If you land in the middle of the catalog with a modest print run announced, the publisher has already communicated their expectations for your book.

Publication Day and the Window That Follows

The first three months after publication are your window. Publishers focus their marketing energy on new releases, and your book is new for exactly that long. After ninety days, attention shifts to the next season's titles. Your book is now backlist, competing for resources against everything the publisher is currently publishing.

Returns are a reality of traditional publishing that self-published authors rarely face. Bookstores buy books on consignment and can return unsold copies. A publisher who ships 5,000 copies to retailers may get 2,000 back. Returns are counted against your royalties. Publishers hold a reserve against returns, meaning they withhold a portion of your earned royalties until they are confident the return period has passed. This reserve is legitimate but means your royalty statements will not reflect your full earnings until twelve to eighteen months after publication.

Royalty statements arrive twice a year for most publishers, covering the period ending six months prior. A book published in January generates a royalty statement in October covering sales through June. You receive that statement and payment in October or November. The lag between when your book earns money and when you see it is built into traditional publishing and cannot be changed.

If your book does not earn back its advance within the first year or two, the publisher will not market it further. They will let it go into natural decline and eventually move it to a print-on-demand model. At that point your book technically remains in print indefinitely, which is why rights reversion clauses matter so much. Without a clear sales threshold triggering reversion, a book earning $200 a year in print-on-demand royalties can tie up your rights for decades.

The Marketing Reality Check

Publishers market books differently than authors expect. Understanding their priorities helps set realistic expectations and guides your own promotional efforts.

Publishers focus marketing budgets on books they expect to succeed, creating a self-fulfilling prophecy. Lead titles get advertising, publicity tours, and bookstore placement. Mid-list titles get basic coverage. Backlist titles get nothing.

Your marketing classification gets determined early in the process based on advance amount, pre-orders, and early reviews. Fight for better classification by delivering strong manuscripts, building pre-publication buzz, and exceeding early sales expectations.

Publishers excel at traditional media placement but often struggle with digital marketing. They can get you newspaper reviews and radio interviews but might fail at social media engagement or online advertising. Plan to supplement their efforts with your own digital strategy.

Bookstore placement depends more on publisher relationships than book quality. Major publishers have sales reps who maintain personal relationships with bookstore buyers. These relationships determine shelf placement, staff recommendations, and promotional opportunities.

Publishers think in terms of seasonal campaigns, not ongoing promotion. Your book gets intensive marketing attention for 3-6 months around publication, then competes with newer releases for promotional resources. Build momentum during your window, then sustain it independently.

When Traditional Publishing Actually Makes Sense

Traditional publishing works best for authors who view books as career investments instead of immediate income sources. The lower royalty rates and long timelines only make sense if you're building toward larger goals.

Choose traditional publishing when credibility matters more than control. Academic authors, business consultants, and professional speakers benefit from publisher validation. A traditionally published book opens doors that self-published books can't access.

Traditional publishing excels for books targeting older demographics who still prefer bookstore shopping and trust publisher recommendations. Literary fiction, serious nonfiction, and books for readers over 50 benefit from traditional distribution and marketing.

Consider traditional publishing when your book requires big upfront investment. Cookbooks with professional photography, technical books with complex illustrations, or books requiring extensive fact-checking justify publisher investment better than author self-funding.

Traditional publishing makes sense when you're writing for long-term backlist sales instead of immediate bestseller success. Publishers keep books in print and available for years, sometimes decades. Self-published authors often struggle to maintain long-term visibility.

The Alternative Paths Nobody Mentions

Smart authors increasingly use hybrid strategies that combine traditional and self-publishing advantages.

Some authors self-publish first to prove market demand, then use sales data to attract traditional publishers. A self-published book that sells 10,000 copies demonstrates commercial viability better than any query letter.

Other authors traditionally publish their main series while self-publishing complementary works. A mystery novelist might traditionally publish novels while self-publishing short story collections or spin-off novellas.

Academic and business authors often traditionally publish flagship books for credibility while self-publishing timely or specialized content. The traditional book establishes authority while self-published works generate ongoing revenue.

Regional authors sometimes start with local publishers to build readership, then use that success to attract national publishers. Local media attention and bookstore relationships provide platform development opportunities.

Is Traditional Publishing Right for You?

Traditional publishing isn't about prestige or validation. It's a business decision that should match your career goals, timeline, and financial needs.

Ask yourself why you want traditional publishing. If the answer involves validation, prestige, or proving yourself as a "real" author, reconsider your motivations. Publishers are business partners, not validators.

Evaluate your timeline honestly. Traditional publishing takes 2-4 years from submission to bookstore. If you need income sooner or want to capitalize on timely topics, traditional publishing won't serve your needs.

Consider your marketing capabilities and preferences. Traditional publishing requires active author participation but provides professional support and industry connections. Self-publishing offers complete control but demands full responsibility for every aspect of book success.

Traditional publishing works for authors who prioritize long-term career development over immediate control and income. It's a strategic choice that requires patience, professionalism, and realistic expectations about both the process and outcomes.

The industry has changed dramatically, but traditional publishing still offers unique advantages for authors whose goals match what publishers capabilities. Make the decision based on strategy, not sentiment.

Chapter 7: Hybrid Publishing

Hybrid publishing sits between traditional and self-publishing. You pay for professional services upfront, but keep your rights and higher royalty rates than traditional publishing offers. Sounds like the best of both worlds. Most hybrid publishers are dressed-up vanity presses that take your money and deliver garbage results.

The hybrid publishing industry is filled with predators who prey on authors' dreams of professional publishing without the rejection and waiting of traditional routes. They promise the prestige of traditional publishing with the control of self-publishing, then deliver amateur services at premium prices.

Legitimate hybrid publishers do exist. They provide genuine professional services, maintain quality standards, and deliver real value for their fees. The trick is telling the difference between legitimate hybrid publishers and expensive vanity presses wearing hybrid costumes.

Expect to pay \$3,000-\$15,000 for hybrid publishing services. If you don't have that budget and can't prove the investment will pay off, stick with self-publishing platforms until you do.

The Economics of Paying to Publish

Hybrid publishing flips the traditional publishing model. Instead of publishers investing in your book and keeping most profits, you invest in professional services and keep most profits. This only makes financial sense if you can sell enough books to recover your investment.

The math is brutal. If you pay \$10,000 for hybrid publishing and earn \$5 profit per book sold, you need to sell 2,000 copies just to break even. Most books sell fewer than 500 copies total. Most hybrid published books lose money for their authors.

Successful hybrid publishing requires realistic sales projections based on your platform, genre, and marketing capabilities. A business consultant with 5,000 email subscribers and regular speaking engagements might sell 2,000 copies of a leadership book. A first-time novelist with no platform probably won't sell 200 copies.

Publishers love authors who don't do this math. They focus on the dream of professional publishing instead of the reality of book sales. Do the math before you sign anything.

The break-even calculation gets worse when you factor in opportunity costs. That $10,000 invested in stocks might generate $1,000 annually in dividends. Your book needs to generate ongoing income, not just recover its initial cost.

Why Most Hybrid Publishers Are Scams

Real hybrid publishers are selective. They reject manuscripts that don't meet their standards, even when authors can pay their fees. Most companies calling themselves "hybrid publishers" are vanity presses that will publish anything for money.

Vanity presses survive by convincing authors that professional-looking results justify amateur content. They'll edit your grammar and design a decent cover, but they can't fix fundamental problems with your book's concept, structure, or market appeal.

The business model explains everything. Vanity presses make money from author fees, not book sales. They have no incentive to ensure your book succeeds in the market. They get paid whether your book sells 10 copies or 10,000 copies.

Legitimate hybrid publishers invest their reputation in every book they publish. They want books that will sell well, get good reviews, and enhance their brand. Vanity presses just want your money.

Ask potential publishers what percentage of submitted manuscripts they reject. Legitimate hybrids reject 70-90% of submissions. Vanity presses reject almost none.

The Credibility Question

Many authors choose hybrid publishing for credibility. They believe hybrid-published books carry more prestige than self-published books. Mostly psychological.

Readers don't care who published your book. They care whether it's good. A well-written, professionally produced self-published book gets better reception than a poorly written hybrid-published book.

Industry professionals might notice the difference, but only if they're familiar with the publisher. Most people can't tell the difference between a high-quality self-published book and a hybrid-published book.

The credibility benefit exists mainly in your own mind and in certain professional contexts. If you're positioning yourself as an expert consultant or speaker, the perceived credibility might justify the cost. For most, it does not.

Real credibility comes from book sales, positive reviews, and reader engagement. Publishers can't manufacture these outcomes for you.

Evaluating Publisher Quality

Research hybrid publishers like you're making a major business investment, because you are.

Look at their published catalog. Do the books look professional? Are they available in bookstores? Do they have good reviews? Are authors active and successful?

Contact recent authors directly. Publishers should provide contact information for authors willing to discuss their experience. **Ask about** service quality, timeline adherence, **marketing effectiveness,** and ongoing support.

Check their distribution claims. Are their books really **available in bookstores** and libraries, or just orderable through **online systems? Walk** into a Barnes & Noble and try to find their titles.

Review their staff credentials. Are their editors published **professionals with relevant** experience? Do their designers have **impressive portfolios?** Are their marketing people former **publishing industry** professionals?

Calculate their pricing against freelance alternatives. A **hybrid package costing** $12,000 should provide services worth **at least $12,000 if** purchased separately. Often you can get **better services for less** money by hiring freelancers directly.

Service Quality Red Flags

Most hybrid publishing problems stem from unrealistic **promises and poor service** delivery.

Guaranteed bestseller claims are bullshit. No publisher can **guarantee sales results.** Books succeed because of content **quality, market timing,** and marketing effectiveness, not **publisher names.**

Celebrity endorsement offers are usually fake. Real **celebrities don't endorse** unknown books for money. If they **offer celebrity endorsements,** ask for names and verification.

Expensive marketing packages often deliver minimal value. **A $5,000 marketing** package might consist of press releases **that nobody reads and** social media posts that generate no **engagement.**

Rush deadlines and limited-time pricing offers are pressure **tactics designed to** prevent careful consideration. Legitimate **publishers don't use car** dealership sales tactics.

Contract Terms That Matter

Hybrid publishing contracts should heavily favor authors since you're paying for services.

You must retain full copyright ownership. Never sign contracts that transfer any rights to publishers. You're paying for services, not selling your book.

Subsidiary rights should remain with you. Movie rights, translation rights, and audio rights belong to authors who pay for publishing services.

Performance standards should be clear and measurable. Vague promises about "professional editing" or "complete marketing" are meaningless. Demand exact deliverables with quality standards and timelines.

Termination clauses should allow you to end the relationship if publishers fail to deliver promised services. You should also retain ownership of all files and materials if the relationship ends.

The Alternative Strategy

Before paying for hybrid publishing, consider building your own professional team.

Hire a developmental editor for $2,000-4,000 to fix structural problems. Hire a copy editor for $1,000-2,000 to clean up grammar and style. Hire a cover designer for $300-800 for a custom cover. Hire a formatter for $200-500 for professional interior design.

Total cost: $3,500-7,300 for services comparable to basic hybrid packages. You maintain complete control and build relationships with professionals you can work with on future books.

The learning curve is steeper, but you develop valuable skills and industry knowledge. You also avoid the markup that hybrid publishers charge for coordinating services you could manage yourself.

Many successful authors start with hybrid publishing, then switch to self-publishing with freelancers once they understand the process. Cut out the middleman from the beginning.

When Hybrid Publishing Makes Sense

Hybrid publishing works for authors who need professional credibility, have realistic sales expectations, and can afford the investment without financial hardship.

Business authors who need credible books for consulting or speaking careers might justify the investment. The book becomes a marketing tool that generates revenue through other channels.

Authors with established platforms and proven audiences can more easily recover hybrid publishing investments. If you already have 10,000 email subscribers or 50,000 social media followers, you have built-in distribution for your book.

Genre matters enormously. Literary fiction and serious nonfiction benefit more from professional presentation than genre fiction. Romance and mystery readers care more about story than publisher prestige.

Time-pressed authors with disposable income might prefer hybrid publishing's convenience over managing freelancers themselves. The all-in-one service delivery can justify premium pricing for busy professionals.

The ROI Reality Check

Most hybrid published books don't generate enough revenue to justify their costs. That doesn't mean hybrid publishing is bad, but it does mean you need realistic expectations.

Calculate your break-even point based on realistic sales projections, not optimistic fantasies. If you need to sell 3,000 copies to break even but have no platform or marketing plan, hybrid publishing is an expensive mistake.

Consider non-monetary returns on investment. Professional credibility, industry connections, and personal satisfaction might justify costs that pure financial analysis wouldn't support.

Think long-term. Your book might not immediately recover its costs but could generate speaking opportunities, consulting clients, or media appearances that provide financial returns over several years.

Factor in learning value. Working with professional editors and designers teaches skills and industry knowledge that benefit future projects.

Finding Legitimate Hybrid Publishers

The Independent Book Publishers Association (IBPA) publishes a hybrid publishing criteria checklist that defines what a legitimate hybrid publisher looks like. The core requirements are these: the publisher must be selective and reject manuscripts. It must pay royalties above industry standard, at least 50% of net for print and at least 70% of net for ebook. It must provide transparent reporting, produce professionally edited and designed books, and distribute through the same channels as traditional publishers. Use this checklist as a filter before you spend a dollar.

The IBPA also maintains a list of members who meet their hybrid publishing criteria. This is not a guarantee of quality, but it eliminates the obvious predators. Inks and Bindings, Greenleaf Book Group, Publish Your Purpose, and She Writes Press are examples of publishers that have met the IBPA standard. They are not cheap and they are selective, but they are operating as described rather than as a sales operation wearing a publisher costume.

Beyond the IBPA list, the Reedsy marketplace is worth knowing. Reedsy is not a hybrid publisher. It is a freelancer marketplace where you can find vetted editors, cover designers, and formatters individually. Using Reedsy to build your own team costs less than a hybrid package and gives you direct relationships with the professionals doing the work. If the hybrid model appeals to you because of the project management convenience, Reedsy offers a middle path.

What Hybrid Publishing Actually Costs

The range of $3,000 to $15,000 covers a lot of territory. Understanding what drives cost helps you evaluate whether a quote is reasonable.

Developmental editing is the most expensive single service. A full developmental edit on a 70,000-word manuscript from an experienced editor runs $2,500 to $5,000 depending on depth and turnaround. If a hybrid package includes developmental editing for $500 more than one without it, the developmental edit is not real.

Cover design from a professional with publishing experience runs $500 to $1,500 for a custom design. Stock photo manipulation dressed up as a cover design runs $150 to $300 and looks like it. The difference is obvious when you put both covers next to traditionally published competitors.

Interior formatting for a standard trade paperback runs $200 to $500. Complex formatting with multiple styles, sidebars, or images costs more. Ebook formatting separately runs $100 to $300. Any hybrid package pricing these services at a significant markup is charging you for coordination, not skill.

Distribution is not a service that justifies cost. IngramSpark and KDP are free to upload to. Any hybrid publisher charging you for access to distribution is charging you for something you can do yourself for nothing. Distribution setup should appear in a hybrid contract as a task, not a line item.

The Self-Publishing Comparison

Before signing with any hybrid publisher, run this exercise. Take their total package price. Go to Reedsy or the Editorial Freelancers Association directory and price out each service separately: developmental edit, copy edit, proofreading, cover design, interior formatting. Add those numbers up. Then compare that total to the hybrid quote.

In most cases the freelancer route costs 20% to 40% less than the hybrid package for equivalent services. You also retain direct relationships with each professional, which means you can hire them again for your next book without going through a middleman.

The argument for the hybrid route is project management: one point of contact, one timeline, one invoice. That convenience is real. It is worth something. The question is whether it is worth a $3,000 premium over doing it yourself, which is roughly what the average markup works out to on legitimate hybrid packages. For a first book from an author who has never managed a publishing project, that might be a fair price for the hand-holding. For anyone with one book already behind them, it probably is not.

Is Hybrid Publishing Right for You?

Choose hybrid publishing when professional presentation matters more than profit maximization and you can afford the investment without financial stress.

Skip hybrid publishing if you're trying to make money from book sales alone. The economics rarely work for authors without established platforms and marketing capabilities.

Avoid hybrid publishing if you can't afford quality services. Cheap hybrid packages often deliver results worse than competent self-publishing.

Consider hybrid publishing as professional development investment instead of immediate income generation. The credibility and industry connections might justify costs that book sales alone can't support.

The hybrid publishing landscape includes both legitimate service providers and skilled scammers. Success requires careful research, realistic expectations, and strategic thinking about your publishing goals. Choose carefully or don't choose at all.

The Author Solutions Problem

One company dominates the predatory hybrid publishing space: Author Solutions, Inc. They operate under dozens of brand names specifically to avoid the bad reputation their main name has built up. AuthorHouse, Xlibris, iUniverse, Trafford Publishing, Archway Publishing (Simon and Schuster's self-publishing imprint), WestBow Press (Thomas Nelson's self-publishing imprint), and Balboa Press (Hay House's self-publishing imprint) are all Author Solutions operations.

The association with major publishers is intentional and misleading. Seeing WestBow Press described as "a division of Thomas Nelson" makes authors believe they are getting traditional publishing quality and connections. They are not. They are paying Author Solutions fees. Thomas Nelson collects a referral payment and has nothing to do with your book.

Author Solutions has been the subject of class action lawsuits over hidden fees, royalty calculation disputes, and misleading sales practices. The lawsuits have produced settlements and ongoing litigation. If a company you are considering turns out to be an Author Solutions brand, stop and walk away regardless of how the sales pitch sounds.

Finding out if a company is an Author Solutions brand takes thirty seconds. Search the company name plus "Author Solutions" and you will find the connection documented in author advocacy resources and industry reporting. Do this before taking any sales call from any hybrid publisher you have not independently verified.

What a Hybrid Publishing Contract Should Include

If you decide a hybrid publisher is right for you, the contract is where most problems originate. A contract that protects you looks substantially different from the standard contracts predatory companies offer.

You retain copyright. The contract should state explicitly that you own the copyright and all rights to your work. The publisher is providing services, not acquiring publishing rights. Any contract that grants the publisher rights to your work in exchange for fees is structured backwards and should be rejected.

All deliverables are specified in writing. "Professional editing" is not a deliverable. "One developmental edit pass with written editorial report, followed by one copy edit pass with corrections provided in tracked changes" is a deliverable. Every service in the package should have a description specific enough that you could verify whether it was delivered.

Timelines are stated and enforceable. The contract should specify when each deliverable will be completed and what happens if the publisher misses deadlines. A contract with no timeline is a contract with no accountability.

You own all production files. When the project is complete, you receive the formatted interior file, the cover design file in its original format, and any other materials created for your book. These files belong to you. A publisher who refuses to provide source files after project completion is holding your book hostage.

Termination rights are clear. You should be able to exit the contract if the publisher fails to deliver as promised, with full return of your files and a partial refund for work not yet done. A contract with no exit clause for publisher non-performance traps you with a company that has no incentive to finish.

Royalty rates are specified by format and distribution channel. "Industry standard royalties" is not a royalty rate. The contract should state: ebook royalty X%, print royalty Y%, wholesale discount Z%. Verify these rates against what you would earn publishing directly through KDP and IngramSpark before signing.

The Timeline Reality of Hybrid Publishing

Reputable hybrid publishers take five to nine months from contract signing to publication. This is slower than self-publishing directly on KDP (which can go live in 48 hours) but faster than traditional publishing. The timeline matters for planning launches, securing advance reviews, and timing market entry.

The typical sequence runs like this. Editorial intake takes two to four weeks after signing. Developmental editing takes six to ten weeks for a full-length book. Author revisions take two to four weeks. Copy editing takes two to three weeks. Cover design runs three to six weeks and overlaps with the later editorial stages. Interior formatting takes two to three weeks after final manuscript approval. Proof review takes one to two weeks. Distribution setup and go-live takes one to four weeks.

If a hybrid publisher promises to publish your book in four to six weeks, that timeline is only achievable if they are cutting corners on editing and design. Quality editorial work takes the time it takes. Speed promises are a red flag for companies that treat publishing as a transaction rather than a craft.

Chapter 8: Alternative Publishing Platforms

Beyond Amazon KDP, Draft2Digital, and the major platforms we've covered, dozens of smaller platforms compete for authors and readers. Most aren't worth your time. Some serve niches well. A few offer unique advantages that might fit your publishing strategy.

This chapter covers the platforms that didn't warrant full chapters but might serve your needs. Don't spread yourself too thin across every platform that exists. Focus on the ones that make sense for your genre, goals, and available time.

Most alternative platforms generate minimal sales compared to Amazon and the major retailers. Consider them supplements to your main distribution strategy, not replacements for it.

Smashwords: The Indie Pioneer That Refuses to Die

I tried Smashwords early on. It was a disaster. Their formatting requirements were extraordinarily specific. They had a document called the Smashwords Style Guide that ran dozens of pages and dictated exactly how your Word file had to be structured before they'd accept it. I spent hours trying to meet their specifications and kept getting rejected. Eventually I deleted everything and gave up.

That was then. Draft2Digital acquired Smashwords in 2022, and the platform still operates separately, but the experience is nothing like the nightmare I remember. Don't let old horror stories about Smashwords put you off. The current tools are dramatically simpler. What remains clunky is the interface. It looks like 2010 because it essentially is. but the formatting requirements are no longer the obstacle they once were.

The direct sales royalty rate of 80% beats every other platform. If you can drive readers to buy directly from Smashwords instead of Amazon or Apple, you keep significantly more money per sale. The challenge is getting readers to change their buying habits.

Smashwords converts your Word document into every ebook format automatically. Upload once, get EPUB, MOBI, PDF, RTF, LRF, PDB, and plain text files. No other platform offers this level of format support.

The coupon system lets you create discount codes for readers, reviewers, and promotional campaigns. You can offer 50% off to your email list or free copies to book bloggers. Amazon and most other platforms don't offer comparable promotional tools.

When Smashwords Is Worth Your Time

Choose Smashwords if you have a dedicated fan base willing to buy directly from your website or if you use coupons heavily in your marketing. The 80% royalty rate can significantly impact your income if you make direct sales work.

Skip Smashwords if you're happy with Draft2Digital's distribution and don't want to learn their formatting requirements. The time investment rarely pays off for authors without strong direct marketing capabilities.

Smashwords works best for authors who treat it as a direct sales platform instead of just another distributor. Link to Smashwords from your website, email signature, and social media to capture sales at the highest royalty rate.

PublishDrive: The Subscription Alternative

PublishDrive is worth knowing as a D2D alternative, especially for authors with a larger catalog generating consistent sales. Founded in 2015, it distributes to over 400 stores worldwide including Amazon, Apple Books, Google Play, Kobo, Barnes and Noble, and a broad range of international retailers and library systems.

The pricing model is what sets it apart. Most aggregators take 10% of each sale. PublishDrive offers that model, but also a flat subscription at around $100 a month where you keep 100% of royalties. For a catalog generating more than $1,000 a month in wide distribution sales, the subscription pays for itself. For authors with a few books earning modest income, the 10% royalty-share model is cheaper.

PublishDrive distributes to Amazon, which D2D does not. That said, uploading directly to KDP gives you better placement and higher royalties than going through an aggregator. For most authors, use KDP directly for Amazon and PublishDrive or D2D for everything else.

Barnes & Noble Press: The Struggling Giant

Barnes & Noble Press is B&N's self-publishing platform for ebooks and print. It's not Amazon. It's not close. But it's a more capable platform than its reputation suggests, and several things about it have improved significantly since the version most authors remember.

The royalty rate is a flat 70% on ebooks, which matches Amazon and beats most aggregators. That was bumped up from a lower tiered structure in 2021, so authors citing old numbers are working from outdated information. Payments arrive 30 days after the month of sale. Print books require your own ISBN, which adds a small step D2D doesn't.

B&N has a promotional program worth knowing about. Their weekly genre newsletters reach around half a million readers, and authors can apply for selected placements. It's not self-serve advertising like Amazon. you apply and they decide, but getting featured in one of those newsletters moves books.

The platform also runs periodic sales events where your books can be included.

Getting your print book into physical B&N stores is theoretically possible but practically rare for indie authors. Don't count on it. The ebook side is where the real opportunity is for most authors.

Setting up B&N Press directly is simple if you have your own ISBN. Create an account at press.barnesandnoble.com, upload your EPUB and cover image, fill in your metadata, and set your price. B&N accepts EPUB and Word documents for ebooks. For print, they accept PDF files in standard trim sizes.

The B&N Nook market has contracted significantly since its peak, but it remains a real market, especially for romance, mystery, and literary fiction readers who prefer not to be inside the Amazon world. Authors who write in those genres and have even a small B&N-native readership benefit from the direct account primarily because of promotional program access. Those newsletter placements drive enough sales in genre fiction to justify the separate account management.

B&N pays on a net 30 basis, meaning you receive payment 30 days after the end of the month in which sales occurred. The payment threshold is lower than KDP's. B&N also allows you to set B&N-exclusive prices, meaning you can run a sale on B&N without changing your price elsewhere. This is useful for B&N promotional applications that require a discounted price without triggering Amazon's price-matching and dropping your Amazon royalty.

If you're already distributing through D2D, B&N is already covered and you don't need to touch it. Going direct makes sense if B&N represents meaningful sales for your genre: romance, mystery, and literary fiction tend to perform better there, and you want access to their promotional programs, which D2D authors don't get directly.

Kobo Writing Life: The International Player

Kobo Writing Life is Kobo's direct publishing platform: ebook-only, no print, free to use, and no exclusivity requirements of any kind. That last point matters more than it sounds. Unlike Kindle Unlimited, Kobo's subscription service (Kobo Plus) lets you opt in without giving up other platforms. You can be in Kobo Plus and on Amazon and everywhere else at the same time. Amazon's model forces a choice; Kobo's doesn't.

Royalties are 70% on books priced $2.99 and above, 45% below that. Unlike Amazon, Kobo doesn't charge file delivery fees, so you keep the full percentage. Small difference per sale, real across a catalog.

The international angle is real and often underestimated. Kobo holds roughly 25% of the Canadian ebook market. In the Netherlands they're dominant. Australia and New Zealand skew toward Apple Books and Kobo rather than Amazon. If you've been writing off Canada as a small market, Kobo's numbers might change your mind.

The promotions tab in your Kobo dashboard lists current promotional opportunities you can apply for. These are selected: themed sales, price-drop campaigns, featured placements. Acceptance isn't guaranteed but the opportunities exist and direct authors get access to promotions that aggregator-distributed authors don't.

If US sales are your primary focus and your genre doesn't have obvious international appeal, Kobo probably won't move the needle on its own. But if you're going wide anyway, adding Kobo direct costs nothing and takes an afternoon.

Setting up a Kobo Writing Life account takes about thirty minutes. Go to kobowritinglife.com, create a publisher account, upload your EPUB and cover, set your price and territories, and publish. Kobo accepts EPUB only. No Word document conversion. If you do not have a properly formatted EPUB, produce one through Calibre or Atticus first.

Kobo Plus is the subscription program to understand before opting in. Unlike Kindle Unlimited, enrolling in Kobo Plus does not require exclusivity and does not lock you in for a specific period. You can opt in or out at any time. The per-read payment rate is lower than the equivalent KU rate in most cases, but you are not giving up any other distribution to receive it. For most authors going wide, enrolling in Kobo Plus is a simple yes.

The Canadian market is the single best reason to take Kobo seriously. Kobo was founded in Canada and has deep retailer relationships there through Indigo Books and Music. Authors who dismiss Canada as a small extension of the US market are leaving real money on the table, particularly in romance, mystery, and literary fiction. Check your D2D or direct Kobo dashboard for territory breakdowns before deciding Kobo is not worth your attention.

Apple Books for Authors: The Premium Market

Apple Books is the second-largest ebook market in the US after Amazon, and it operates completely differently. There's no author advertising platform. You can't buy visibility. Human editors choose what gets featured, and those features drive real sales. That means your cover, your category placement, and the quality of your book page matter more than your ad budget.

The royalty structure has a real advantage over Amazon: 70% on every sale at any price point, no upper limit. Amazon drops you to 35% on books priced above $9.99. Apple doesn't have that ceiling, which makes box sets and premium-priced nonfiction significantly more profitable there.

Apple's pre-order system works differently too. Pre-order sales count toward your launch-day sales rank rather than being spread across the pre-order period. If you get 50 pre-orders, those 50 sales hit your ranking on day one, which is the opposite of how Amazon handles it. For authors who build launch teams and drive early orders, this compounds the visibility effect at exactly the right moment.

No Mac required. This was true years ago but Apple launched a web-based publishing portal that works on any computer. The setup requires an Apple ID and an EPUB file, not a Word document conversion. That's the main technical ask. If you can produce an EPUB, you can publish direct.

D2D covers Apple if you're already distributing wide, and for most authors that's enough to start. Going direct makes sense once Apple represents a real chunk of your revenue and you want control over pricing changes, metadata updates, and access to their promotional application process, which direct authors can pursue and aggregator authors can't.

Setting up Apple Books for Authors requires an Apple ID and an EPUB file. Go to authors.apple.com and create your account. The submission interface asks for your EPUB, cover image, and metadata separately. Apple's metadata requirements are strict. Your EPUB must pass their validation or it will be rejected at upload. Run your EPUB through an EPUB validator before submitting. Calibre's built-in validator or the free EPUB Validator at epubvalidator.org both work.

Apple Books pays 70% royalty at any price point with no ceiling, monthly, on a net 30 basis after the month of sale. There is no payment threshold. Any amount earned gets paid. For box sets and premium-priced nonfiction priced above $9.99, Apple's unlimited 70% rate produces meaningfully higher per-sale income than Amazon's 35%.

Google Play Books

Google Play Books is one of the five major ebook retailers and the one most authors ignore. That is a mistake, especially for nonfiction. Google Play integrates with Google Search in ways that other platforms do not. Books sold through Google

Play can appear directly in search results, which gives them discoverability that comes from outside the reading world.

Publishing directly on Google Play requires a Google Play Books Partner Center account. Go to play.google.com/books/publish and sign in with a Google account. Google accepts EPUB and PDF. EPUB is preferred for reflowable content. PDF is appropriate for books where layout is fixed, like workbooks or heavily designed nonfiction.

The royalty rate is 70% of your list price, paid monthly. Google sets a minimum price of $0.99 for paid books. You can also make books free on Google Play, which is useful for permafree first-in-series titles. Google processes payments to your bank account once your balance reaches $1 USD, so even small sales pay out promptly.

One Google Play-specific feature worth knowing: Google scans your book content to improve their search indexing. This is how your book can appear in Google Search results related to its subject matter. A well-written nonfiction book on a specific topic can generate organic discoverability through Google Search that no other retailer provides. For practical nonfiction and how-to books, this alone justifies a Google Play account.

D2D does not distribute to Google Play. IngramSpark does not distribute to Google Play. If you want your ebook on Google Play, you must publish there directly. This is the one major retail gap in the standard wide distribution setup and the main reason authors going wide should set up a Google Play account even if they use D2D for every other platform.

Genre-Specific Platforms: Niche Opportunities

Some platforms serve certain genres or content types that mainstream platforms handle poorly.

Radish Fiction focuses on serialized fiction with micropayment models. Readers pay small amounts per chapter, creating ongoing revenue streams for engaging stories. The model works best for authors who can write compelling cliffhangers and maintain regular publishing schedules.

Wattpad provides free fiction platform with a large young adult audience. Authors build followings by publishing chapters regularly and engaging with readers. Success on Wattpad can lead to traditional publishing contracts or adaptation opportunities.

Royal Road serves fantasy and LitRPG fiction communities. The audience is passionate about certain subgenres that mainstream platforms often ignore. Authors can build dedicated followings in these niches.

These platforms rarely generate significant direct income but can build audiences for particular types of content. Think of them as marketing channels instead of primary income sources.

International Platforms: Global Reach

International platforms matter if you target certain countries or languages, but most don't justify the effort for English-language authors focused on US/UK markets.

Storytel dominates audiobook subscriptions in Europe. If you produce audiobooks and target European markets, direct distribution might generate more revenue than going through aggregators.

StreetLib: European and International Distribution

StreetLib is an Italian aggregator worth knowing for authors targeting non-English markets or European readers. Where D2D is built primarily around the US and UK ebook market, StreetLib has deeper relationships in Europe, Latin America, and South Asia. They distribute to over 50 partners including Storytel, BookBeat, and Nextory in the Nordic markets, and have reach in Germany, Italy, Spain, and Portuguese-language markets that D2D does not match.

The fee is 10% commission, same as D2D. They support ebooks, audiobooks, comics, and magazines. Their dashboard is available in English, Italian, Spanish, and Hindi. They also have a short-run print program for quantities as low as 100 copies.

For US and UK authors writing in English for primarily American and British readers, D2D covers the same territory adequately and is easier to use. StreetLib becomes relevant when your book has a real European or Latin American audience, when you are publishing in another language, or when you want the widest possible international footprint and are willing to manage a second aggregator account to get it.

Audiobooks: Production and Distribution

Audiobook consumption has grown every year for a decade and shows no sign of reversing. If your book is not in audio, you are invisible to a large segment of readers who primarily consume books through their ears. This section covers production options and distribution decisions. The marketing side is covered in the companion volume, Sell Your Books.

The Production Decision

You have three options: hire a narrator, offer a royalty share deal, or use AI narration.

Hiring a narrator outright means paying per finished hour, typically $150 to $400 for professional narrators. A 60,000-word novel runs roughly 6 to 7 hours of finished audio. Budget $900 to $2,800 depending on the narrator. You own the audio outright, keep 100% of royalties, and can distribute anywhere. This is the most expensive option upfront and the best deal long-term for books likely to sell consistently.

Royalty share means the narrator produces the book for free in exchange for 50 percent of royalties, typically locked in for seven years. It eliminates upfront cost but is often more expensive long-term. ACX (Amazon's Audiobook Creation Exchange) is the primary marketplace for finding narrators and arranging royalty share deals.

AI narration has become commercially viable. Tools like ElevenLabs can narrate a full novel for under $100 at quality levels usable for most commercial fiction and practical nonfiction. AI narration is not appropriate for every book. Memoirs and literary fiction are better served by human voice. For genre fiction and how-to nonfiction, the cost difference is hard to argue with.

The Distribution Decision

The core decision mirrors wide vs. KDP Select for ebooks: ACX exclusivity versus wide audiobook distribution.

ACX distributes to Audible, Amazon, and Apple Books. Enrolling exclusively through ACX locks you in for seven years, not a 90-day term like KDP Select, but a seven-year commitment. Exclusive ACX pays 40% royalties. Non-exclusive pays 25%. Think carefully before committing.

Going wide means distributing to Audible, Apple Books, Kobo, Hoopla, OverDrive, and dozens of other platforms with no exclusivity requirement. Voices by INaudio, formerly Findaway Voices, rebranded in August 2025, is the standard wide audiobook aggregator. One upload reaches all major platforms. The royalty split is 80/20 in the author's favor with no exclusivity locked in.

Chirp, BookBub's audiobook platform, is available to books distributed wide. ACX-exclusive titles cannot participate.

Practical recommendation: if you already distribute ebooks wide, distribute audiobooks wide through Voices by INaudio. If you are KDP Select and your genre performs strongly on Audible, use ACX non-exclusive at 25% as a starting point. Never take ACX exclusive without running the seven-year math first.

24symbols serves Spanish and Latin American ebook markets. Authors with content relevant to these markets might find dedicated audiences willing to pay premium prices.

Gumroad: Platform Risk Worth Knowing

Gumroad is a simple platform for selling digital products directly, including ebooks. This is not a recommendation but a warning.

Selling Directly to Readers

Every platform covered in this book takes a percentage of your sale. KDP takes 30 to 65 percent. IngramSpark takes printing costs, a wholesale discount, and a market access fee. D2D takes 10 percent of list price. Selling directly from your own website eliminates all of that. You set the price, you process the payment, you deliver the file, and you keep roughly 95 to 97 percent of every sale after payment processing fees.

The infrastructure for direct ebook sales has three components: a storefront where readers can browse and buy, a payment processor, and a delivery system that sends the file to the customer. You do not need to build any of this yourself.

Payhip is the simplest option. Create a free account at payhip.com, upload your EPUB and cover, set a price, and you have a product page you can link to. Payhip handles payment processing and sends the download link to the customer automatically. They take 5% of each sale on the free plan, 2% on the Plus plan, and zero on the Pro plan for a monthly fee. For authors making more than a few hundred dollars a month in direct sales, the Pro plan pays for itself quickly.

BookFunnel handles the delivery side specifically well. Authors upload their ebook files to BookFunnel, and BookFunnel sends readers a landing page with device-specific download instructions. This dramatically reduces the support burden from customers who cannot figure out how to get an EPUB onto their Kindle. BookFunnel integrates with Payhip, Shopify, WooCommerce, and most major email platforms. It costs $20 to $150 per year depending on your plan and sales volume.

Shopify and WooCommerce are full e-commerce platforms that can sell books alongside merchandise, courses, and anything else you want to offer. They are more powerful and more complex than Payhip, and they make sense once your direct sales operation is large enough to justify the setup time. Authors starting with direct sales should begin with Payhip and graduate to Shopify when they have proven the channel works for their audience.

The limitation of direct sales is that readers have to find your store. Retailers like Amazon have millions of browsers already looking for books. Your website does not. Direct sales work best for authors who have built an email list or who have an existing audience that trusts them enough to buy outside Amazon's familiar checkout. Starting direct sales before you have an audience typically produces minimal results regardless of the platform you use.

Print book direct sales require more infrastructure. You either hold inventory and ship orders yourself, or you use a print-on-demand service that drop-ships to customers. Lulu Direct allows you to embed a buy button on your website that routes through Lulu's print-on-demand fulfillment. The royalty is lower than selling your own inventory, but the operational simplicity makes it the right starting point for most authors exploring direct print sales.

In 2024, Gumroad introduced AI moderation through a tool called iffy.com. Since then, accounts have been suspended and permanently terminated without warning or explanation. Gumroad's response to affected sellers is that they cannot disclose reasons due to their internal rules. There is no appeal process. Pending royalties at termination are not released.

My account was terminated in January 2025. No reason given. I contacted support. No appeal. No access to funds. The account was gone.

If you use Gumroad, export your customer data regularly and do not let royalties accumulate there. Payhip is a cleaner alternative with a better track record for legitimate sellers.

Chapter 9: Offset Printing and Commercial Print Runs

Print-on-demand changed self-publishing by removing the requirement to commit cash upfront to a pile of books that might or might not sell. For most indie authors most of the time, POD is the right answer. But not always.

I had a client who needed 3,000 copies of a business book for a corporate rollout. He was based on an island in the Pacific, and when he priced out shipping that quantity of books from the US mainland, the freight cost was more than the cost to print them locally. So that is what he did. He found a commercial printer on the island, had the books produced there, and distributed them without ever putting them on a container ship.

The books cost him less per unit than KDP would have charged for US-based print-on-demand, looked better, and solved the logistics problem entirely.

The lesson was not that offset can be cheaper than POD. It was that the right printing decision depends on where the books are going, not just how many you need.

Offset printing is how most books in the world are actually made. A printing plate is created for each page, ink is applied to the plate and transferred to a rubber blanket, and the blanket presses the image onto paper at high speed. The setup cost is significant, which is why it only makes financial sense in volume. Once you have covered setup, the cost per additional unit drops sharply. At 5,000 copies, offset printing produces a better book at a lower per-unit cost than any print-on-demand service.

When Offset Printing Makes Sense

The economics are the deciding factor. Offset printing has high fixed setup costs and low variable costs per unit. POD has zero setup costs and higher variable costs per unit. The break-even point where offset becomes cheaper than POD is typically somewhere between 500 and 1,500 copies depending on trim size, page count, and paper stock.

Offset makes sense when you have a guaranteed buyer for a large quantity. Corporate books ordered for internal distribution, textbooks adopted for a course, books sold in bulk to a conference or organization, books you will sell from the trunk of your car at speaking events for years. If you know you will move the quantity, the economics reward you.

Offset also makes sense when print quality requirements exceed what POD can deliver. Coffee table books, art books, photography collections, and cookbooks with full-bleed color photography on every spread often look better offset on premium stock than they do through KDP or IngramSpark. Commercial printers offer paper stocks, binding options, and finishing treatments that POD platforms simply do not.

Do not go offset for a book you hope will sell. Go offset for a book you know will move. The difference between those two situations is several thousand dollars of risk.

Finding a Commercial Printer

Commercial book printers range from national operations that handle major publishers to regional shops that serve local businesses. For most indie authors pursuing offset, the mid-tier national printers offer the best combination of quality, price transparency, and experience with book publishing specifications.

Thomson-Shore, Sheridan Books, McNaughton and Gunn, and Bookmasters are established US printers with experience in trade books. They can advise on paper selection, binding options, and file requirements. They also have relationships with freight companies and can coordinate delivery to a warehouse or fulfillment center. For international print runs, companies like Friesens in Canada and various printers in China and India handle large quantities at lower per-unit costs, though lead times are longer and minimum quantities are typically higher.

A print broker is an intermediary who manages relationships with multiple printers and can source competitive bids for your project. If you are not familiar with the printing industry, a print broker can save you from expensive specification errors and get you better pricing than you would negotiate alone. Their fee is typically built into the quote rather than charged separately. Ask other authors or publishers in your network for referrals to brokers they trust.

Get quotes from at least three sources before committing. Printing quotes depend on quantity, trim size, page count, paper weight, binding type, color vs. black and white, lamination, and delivery location. A change in any of these variables changes the price significantly. Get all quotes based on identical specifications so you are comparing apples to apples.

File Requirements and Proofing

Commercial printers typically require the same file types as IngramSpark: print-ready PDF for interior and cover, 300 DPI minimum for images, CMYK color mode for color content, with correct bleed and crop marks. The difference is that commercial printers often have stricter specifications and less tolerance for minor deviations than POD platforms. Ask for their preflight checklist before you submit files and have a professional designer or print-experienced formatter review your files before submission.

The proofing process is more involved than POD. Commercial printers typically offer a digital proof, a PDF rendering of how the book will print, and optionally a physical press proof, which is an actual printed and bound copy produced before the full run begins. A press proof costs extra but is essential for color-critical books. Approve the digital proof for layout and text accuracy. Approve the press proof for color, paper feel, and binding quality. Do not approve either without reviewing every page.

Changes after press approval are expensive. Unlike POD where you can upload a corrected file at any time, offset corrections after press approval may require new plates and can delay the entire print run. Get the files right before you submit, and review the proof as carefully as you reviewed your manuscript.

Paper, Binding, and Finishing Options

Commercial printers offer substantially more production options than POD platforms. This is one of the reasons authors with specific quality requirements choose offset.

Paper options include the standard 50# and 60# offset stocks used by most trade publishers, premium 70# stocks for heavier, higher-quality feel, coated stocks for photo-heavy books, and specialty options including recycled, acid-free archival, and various colored stocks. Your printer can send paper samples before you commit to a stock.

Binding options go beyond the perfect binding (glued spine) of most POD books. Smyth-sewn binding sews signatures together before gluing, producing a book that opens flatter and lasts longer. PUR adhesive binding uses a stronger glue than standard perfect binding and is more durable for books that will be opened frequently. Lay-flat binding allows pages to open completely flat, essential for workbooks, planners, and reference books. Case binding is hardcover. Spiral and coil binding are available for workbooks and manuals.

Finishing options include matte and gloss lamination on covers, soft-touch matte for a premium feel, spot UV coating that applies a glossy finish to specific elements on a matte cover, foil stamping for metallic titles or design elements, embossing and debossing for textured cover effects, and edge painting for decorative page edges on hardcovers. These treatments add cost but can make a book into a premium product that commands a higher price and serves as a physical object readers want to own.

The Economics of a Print Run

Commercial printing quotes are always quantity-dependent. The unit cost at 500 copies will be significantly higher than at 5,000 copies because the setup costs are spread over more units. Request quotes at multiple quantities to understand your cost curve.

As a rough reference for a standard 6 by 9 trade paperback, 200 pages, black and white interior, the unit cost at 500 copies typically runs $4 to $7. At 1,000 copies, $3 to $5. At 2,500 copies, $2 to $4. At 5,000 copies, $1.50 to $3. These figures vary with paper choice, binding, and shipping. Color interiors add $2 to $5 per unit at most quantities. Get actual quotes for your specific specifications rather than relying on estimates.

Factor in all costs when calculating viability: printing, freight to your warehouse or storage location, storage costs if you are using a fulfillment house, and the cost of any unsold inventory if the run does not move. The per-unit printing cost is only part of the real cost of a print run.

Storage, Fulfillment, and Distribution

This is the part of offset printing that surprises authors most. When your 3,000 books arrive on a pallet, someone has to receive them, store them, pick them, pack them, and ship them to buyers. That operation does not exist by default.

Before you choose an option, understand what the operation actually requires. When a retailer or reader orders your book, someone has to pull it from a shelf or bin, check the quantity and condition, pack it into a box with appropriate protection, print a shipping label, and hand it to a carrier. That chain of actions is fulfillment.

It sounds simple when described in a sentence. It is less simple when you are doing it for the fortieth order this week while also trying to write your next book.

Your options are: store and fulfill yourself, use a fulfillment house, or use Amazon FBA.

Storing and fulfilling yourself means your garage, basement, or office becomes a warehouse. For small quantities and direct sales at events, this is manageable. For ongoing retail orders, it becomes a full-time logistics operation quickly. Packing and shipping individual orders is time-consuming work that takes you away from writing.

Fulfillment houses receive your inventory, store it in their warehouse, and ship orders on your behalf when they come in. They charge per unit stored and per unit shipped. For authors with steady order volume, a fulfillment house is worth the cost.

Ingram Publisher Services, Independent Publishers Group (IPG), and Consortium are established options that also offer distribution services, getting your book into retail ordering systems so stores can find and order it. Working with a distributor typically requires a minimum catalog size and a track record of sales, and new authors may not qualify immediately.

Amazon FBA (Fulfillment by Amazon) accepts author inventory and stores it in Amazon warehouses. When a customer orders on Amazon, Amazon picks, packs, and ships. Your book gets Prime eligibility, which improves conversion significantly. The fees include storage and fulfillment per unit. FBA is worth considering if your offset-printed book is also listed on KDP and you want Amazon to handle the physical fulfillment while you direct buyers there.

Getting offset-printed books into bookstores without a distributor relationship requires contacting store buyers directly. Independent bookstores will often carry local authors on consignment. Chains require distributor relationships to place orders through their systems. This is one reason offset printing makes most sense for books with a defined buyer: a corporate client, a specific organization, or a conference, rather than general retail distribution, which requires infrastructure most indie authors do not have.

Working With Your Printer

Your relationship with a commercial printer benefits from clear communication from the start. Before requesting a quote, know your specifications: trim size, page count, paper stock preference, binding type, cover finish, quantity, and delivery address. Printers quote on specifics. Vague requests produce vague quotes that fall apart at contract stage.

Request a sample book from your printer before you commit. Most established book printers will send a sample from their standard stock at no charge or minimal charge. Hold it, open it, look at the print quality, feel the paper. This is the quality level your book will be produced at. If the sample disappoints you, that printer is not the right choice.

Once you have chosen a printer, you will work with a customer service rep or account manager assigned to your project. Ask them to review your file specifications before you submit final files. Ask them to walk you through their preflight checklist. Printers see the same errors repeatedly and a good rep will tell you what trips up first-time offset customers before it trips you up.

The production timeline at an established US book printer typically runs: file submission and preflight two to five business days; digital proof review two to three business days; press proof production and shipping one to two weeks if ordered; press approval to completion two to four weeks for a standard run; freight to destination, variable. Plan for six to eight weeks from file submission to books in hand. International runs, especially from Asia, take twelve to sixteen weeks or longer once freight is factored in.

International and Local Printing

Printing locally is underused by authors who default to US-based platforms out of habit rather than economics. Every major city in the world has commercial printers. Most of them produce books. The question is whether their quality and pricing compete with shipping books from elsewhere.

For authors based outside North America, Europe, or Australia, local printing frequently wins on total cost. The per-unit printing cost may be higher than a US printer, but once you add international freight, which for a pallet of books can run hundreds to thousands of dollars, local production is often cheaper and always faster.

Finding a local commercial printer is simple. Search for book printers in your city or region. Ask at local print shops whether they handle book production or can refer you. Contact your country's printing industry association for a member directory.

If you are in a smaller market, a short-run digital printer, inkjet or laser rather than offset plates, may be the practical option for quantities under 500 copies. Digital short-run quality has improved dramatically and meets most authors' needs at quantities where offset setup costs are not justified.

When working with a local printer unfamiliar with US publishing standards, bring your own specifications. Provide: trim size in both inches and millimeters, bleed requirements (0.125 inches / 3.175mm on all sides), required resolution (300 DPI minimum), color mode (CMYK for color, grayscale for black and white), and binding type with an example book if possible. The more specific your brief, the more accurate the quote and the fewer surprises in production.

Managing Inventory and Unsold Stock

The risk nobody discusses when recommending offset printing is unsold inventory. Print-on-demand eliminates this risk entirely: you never print more than one copy at a time and you never have stock sitting in a warehouse depreciating. Offset printing reintroduces this risk. If you print 2,000 copies and sell 800, you have 1,200 copies somewhere costing you storage fees and representing cash you will not recover.

Manage this risk before you print, not after. Start with the minimum viable quantity. If the break-even analysis works at 1,000 copies, do not print 3,000 because the per-unit cost is lower. The money you save per unit does not offset the money you lose on inventory you cannot sell. Print what you are confident you can move within twelve months and go back to press for a second run if you need more.

Unsold books have options. Remainder dealers purchase publisher overstock at cents on the dollar. Charitable donations generate tax write-offs in some jurisdictions. Corporate clients sometimes buy remainders for bulk distribution. None of these recovers your full investment, but they are better than books rotting in storage.

When to Return to POD

Offset printing is not a permanent commitment. Many authors run an initial offset print run for a launch or a specific sales opportunity, then switch to POD for ongoing sales.

This hybrid approach makes sense when you need quantity for a launch event or bulk sale and then expect steady but modest ongoing sales; or when the economics of offset justified a first run but ongoing volume does not justify repeat runs.

The switch to POD after an offset run is simple. Your files are already prepared to professional print standards and will pass KDP and IngramSpark file review without problems. The per-unit cost goes back up, but you eliminate inventory risk and storage costs and keep the book available indefinitely.

Chapter 10: Publishing Scams and How to Avoid Them

The publishing industry is crawling with scammers who prey on authors' dreams and inexperience. They promise bestseller status, celebrity endorsements, major media coverage, and guaranteed sales. What they deliver is amateur services, inflated invoices, and broken promises.

These predators target new authors who don't understand how publishing works. They exploit hopes of fame and fortune while delivering services worth a fraction of what they charge. Some are outright thieves who take your money and disappear. Others are incompetent companies that genuinely try but lack the skills to deliver professional results.

This chapter covers the most common publishing scams and how to spot them before they steal your money. Learn to recognize red flags, ask the right questions, and protect yourself from predatory companies that profit from author desperation.

The basic rule: if it sounds too good to be true, it is. No legitimate publisher guarantees bestseller status or promises certain sales numbers. Professional publishing services cost thousands of dollars and take months to deliver quality results.

The Vanity Press Evolution

Traditional vanity presses have evolved into slick marketing operations that prey on author vanity and inexperience.

Modern vanity presses don't look like the obvious scams of the past. They have professional websites, polished sales presentations, and testimonials from satisfied customers.

They've learned to sound legitimate while delivering worthless services.

The business model hasn't changed. They make money from author fees, not book sales. They have no incentive to help your book succeed because they're already paid. Success metrics that matter to authors (sales, reviews, readership) are irrelevant to their business model.

AuthorHouse, Xlibris, iUniverse, Trafford Publishing, and Outskirts Press are the biggest names in this space. They're not illegal, but they charge premium prices for amateur services you can get much cheaper elsewhere.

These companies target authors through targeted sales campaigns. They buy lists of people who've searched for publishing information online, then follow up with professional-looking emails and phone calls. The initial contact feels personal. It follows the same script they use on thousands of authors.

The Psychology of Author Exploitation

Scammers understand author psychology better than authors understand publishing business realities.

How to Verify a Publisher in Fifteen Minutes

You do not need to be an industry expert to spot a predatory publisher. You need fifteen minutes and the willingness to do basic research before you get on a sales call.

Search the company name plus the word "complaints," "scam," and "lawsuit." Do this before you look at their website. If the first page of results is full of author forums warning about them, that is your answer. Predatory publishers generate consistent complaint patterns across multiple unrelated sources. One complaint might be a disgruntled author. Twenty complaints across a decade of forums is a pattern.

Search the company name plus "Author Solutions." Many predatory publishers are Author Solutions brands operating under different names. The connection is documented. If you find it, stop the conversation.

Go to the Association of Authors' Representatives (aaronline.org) and search for the agent or agency by name. Legitimate agents are not always AAR members, but agents not listed anywhere in verifiable industry databases are a red flag. Search QueryTracker and Publishers Marketplace for the agent's name and recent sales. A legitimate agent has a public record of actual deals with actual publishers.

Call their phone number from their website. Predatory operations frequently have numbers that go to voicemail or are disconnected. A company charging $15,000 for publishing services should be reachable by phone during business hours.

Ask for the names and contact information of three recent clients. Legitimate publishers and service providers give you this without hesitation. A company that cannot provide client references, or that gives you references you cannot independently verify and contact, has something to hide.

Look up the books they claim to have published on Amazon and IngramSpark. Check the publication dates, the reviews, and the sales rank. A publisher whose books nobody reads is showing you exactly what will happen to yours.

What a Fake Contract Actually Looks Like

Predatory contracts are designed to look legitimate to someone who has never seen a publishing contract. They use real legal language, reference real industry terms, and bury the problems in clauses authors do not know to look for.

The rights clause is where most predatory contracts expose themselves. A legitimate self-publishing service contract grants you all rights to your work and specifies that the service provider has no claim to your book after the engagement ends.

A predatory contract may grant the company the right to publish your book "in perpetuity throughout the universe in all formats now known or hereafter developed." That language belongs in a traditional publishing deal, not a service agreement. If a company charging you money also wants your rights, walk away.

The royalty clause in a predatory contract often hides fees. "Author receives 50% of net proceeds" sounds reasonable until you read the definition of net: gross revenue minus printing costs, distribution fees, marketing expenses, administrative costs, platform fees, and any other expenses the publisher determines. Net can be defined so broadly that it approaches zero regardless of what the book earns. Ask for the exact definition of net in writing before you sign anything.

The deliverables clause in a predatory contract is vague by design. "Professional editing" has no enforceable definition. "Comprehensive marketing campaign" means nothing without specifics. "Wide distribution" does not mean bookstores will stock your book. It means your book will be listable in ordering systems, which is true of any IngramSpark title. If the contract does not say exactly what will be delivered, by when, and how you can measure it, you have no recourse when they fail to deliver. That is by design.

The termination clause in a predatory contract often has no exit for the author. You can terminate for convenience, but you lose your deposit. The company can terminate for any reason and keep your money. There is no clause allowing you to terminate if they fail to deliver on time.

A legitimate service contract allows the client to exit if the provider fails to perform as agreed, with a partial refund for work not yet done. If the contract has no such provision, it was not written to protect you.

Authors want validation more than money. Scammers exploit this by offering the appearance of traditional publishing (someone else invests in your book) combined with self-publishing benefits (you keep rights and control). This combination doesn't exist in legitimate publishing.

The emotional manipulation starts with artificial urgency. "We can only accept a limited number of authors this month." "This special pricing expires Friday." "Our editors are excited about your manuscript and want to move quickly." All designed to prevent careful research and comparison shopping.

Scammers create detailed stories about your book's potential. They'll claim editors are "excited" about your manuscript after reading a brief synopsis. They'll suggest your book could become a bestseller with the right marketing support. They present their expensive services as investments in guaranteed success.

The victims aren't stupid. They're hopeful people who've worked hard on something they care about. The scammers understand this emotional state and use it against them.

Fake Literary Agents: The Gatekeeping Scam

Scam agents prey on authors desperate for traditional publishing representation.

Real literary agents work on commission only. They earn money when you earn money. Fake agents demand upfront fees for reading manuscripts, editing services, submission packages, or marketing materials.

The most convincing fake agents offer representation contracts with hidden fees and obligations. They'll claim relationships with publishers they've never worked with and promise submission opportunities that don't exist.

Legitimate agents have verifiable sales to real publishers. They can name editors they work with and provide references from other authors they represent. Many belong to the Association of Authors' Representatives, which has ethical standards and professional requirements.

Ask potential agents for their recent sales list, contact information for current clients, and editors they work with regularly. Real agents provide this information readily. Fake agents make excuses or provide vague responses.

The editing service scam is the worst of these. Fake agents will offer representation contingent on expensive editing services from their "preferred" editor. This looks like real representation. It is a way to collect editing fees before the fake agent disappears.

Marketing Scams: Selling Hope Instead of Results

Marketing scammers promise massive exposure and guaranteed sales through expensive promotional packages.

The social media follower scam sells fake engagement that platforms detect and remove. Buying 10,000 Twitter followers sounds impressive until you realize they're all bots that never interact with your content or buy your books.

Blog tour services charge hundreds of dollars to arrange appearances on low-traffic blogs with no engaged audiences. You'll get a schedule that looks impressive but generates zero sales or real exposure.

Publicity campaigns promise press releases to thousands of media outlets but deliver form letters that journalists immediately delete. Real media coverage requires personalized pitches, established relationships, and newsworthy content.

Celebrity endorsement services claim connections to famous people who've never heard of the company. They'll take your money, then deliver endorsements from unknown people with impressive-sounding titles.

Bestseller campaign packages promise to manipulate sales rankings through coordinated buying campaigns. These tactics violate platform terms of service and can result in account penalties for participating authors.

The Fake Review Economy

Review scammers promise positive reviews from "professional reviewers" or "industry experts."

Platforms like Amazon and Goodreads have detection systems for fake reviews. Accounts that consistently leave positive reviews for books from the same companies get flagged and removed. The reviews disappear along with any perceived benefit.

Fake review sites create professional-looking websites with made-up reviewers who have impressive credentials but don't exist. These "reviews" provide no credibility because nobody recognizes the reviewing organization.

Review exchange programs require you to write fake reviews for other books in exchange for fake reviews of your book. This violates platform terms of service and risks getting your account banned from major retailers.

The damage from fake reviews extends beyond wasted money. Getting caught buying fake reviews destroys your credibility with readers, reviewers, and the industry. The short-term appearance of success creates long-term reputation damage.

Contest and Award Manipulation

Fake contests prey on authors' desire for recognition and credibility.

Pay-to-play contests charge entry fees for awards that everyone wins. The business model depends on entry fees, not selective recognition of excellence. They'll create multiple award categories to ensure every entrant receives something.

These fake contests use impressive names and claim celebrity judges who've never heard of the contest. They sell expensive plaques, certificates, and marketing materials to "winners" who paid for recognition.

Legitimate contests are usually free to enter and have established reputations among authors and publishers. They award prizes selectively and provide real recognition that industry professionals respect.

Winners of legitimate contests can name previous winners, describe judging criteria, and explain what benefits the recognition provided. Fake contest winners can't provide this information because it doesn't exist.

Service Quality Scams

Editing and design scammers charge premium prices for amateur work.

The extremely low price editing scam promises professional editing for $200-500. These services use non-native English speakers or automated tools that miss context, tone, and nuance issues that professional editors catch.

The extremely high price editing scam charges $10,000+ for services that freelance professionals provide for $2,000-4,000. These companies exploit authors who equate higher prices with better quality.

Design scammers sell custom covers but deliver generic templates available elsewhere for free. They use obviously amateur stock photos or overused images that appear on dozens of other books.

Professional editors and designers provide portfolios, client references, and sample work before requesting payment. They communicate clearly about timelines, deliverables, and revision policies.

Financial Protection Strategies

Protect your money and rights when working with any publishing service provider.

Use credit cards for all publishing purchases to enable chargebacks if services aren't delivered. Avoid wire transfers, cryptocurrency, or other payment methods that can't be reversed.

Pay for services in milestones tied to deliverable completion instead of large upfront payments. This ensures you receive value before paying and limits losses if relationships go bad.

Include exact deliverables and timelines in all contracts. Vague promises about "professional editing" or "complete marketing" can't be enforced if disputes arise.

Retain ownership of all files and materials created for your projects. Source files, design elements, and content should belong to you regardless of service provider relationships.

Due Diligence That Works

Research service providers like you're making major business investments, because you are.

Questions a Scammer Cannot Answer

Every predatory publisher has a script. They know how to handle the obvious questions because those questions come up constantly. These questions get past the script:

Name three books you have published in the last twelve months that have sold more than 500 copies. Provide the Amazon ASINs. A legitimate publisher knows their catalog's sales performance. A predatory publisher does not track sales because sales are not their business model.

What is your rejection rate? What percentage of manuscripts submitted to you do you decline to publish? Legitimate hybrid publishers and small presses reject the majority of submissions. A company that publishes everything that comes with a check is a vanity press regardless of what they call themselves.

Show me a royalty statement from a book you published in the last year. Redact the author's name. A legitimate publisher can show you what the financial relationship looks like in practice. A predatory publisher will tell you this information is confidential.

What editor will work on my book, and what are their credentials? Not the company's general editorial team. The specific person who will edit my manuscript. What have they published? Who are their previous clients? Can I speak with them before I sign?

What happens to my files when our agreement ends? Do I receive the formatted interior file, the cover design in its original format, and all other materials produced for my book? Or do those files remain your property? The answer tells you everything about whose interests the contract serves.

Check business registration, Better Business Bureau ratings, and complaint history with state consumer protection agencies. Legitimate businesses have clean records and proper licensing.

Contact previous clients directly to ask about service quality, timeline adherence, and overall satisfaction. Real service providers provide client references willingly.

Research online reviews across multiple platforms for consistent feedback patterns. Single positive reviews on company websites mean nothing compared to consistent feedback across independent review sites.

Ask for examples of successful projects in your genre with measurable results. Marketing companies should show you real numbers from past campaigns: traffic, sales, and results.

Recovery from Publishing Scams

If you've been scammed, take immediate action to minimize damage and recover what you can.

Cancel all recurring payments immediately and document everything: communications, contracts, and payment records. This evidence supports dispute resolution and potential legal action.

Contact your credit card company to report fraudulent charges and request chargebacks. Credit card companies often side with consumers in disputes with service providers who don't deliver promised services.

File complaints with the Better Business Bureau, Federal Trade Commission, and state attorney general offices. These complaints create official records that warn other consumers and may trigger investigations.

Share your experience with other authors through online forums and writing communities. Your warning helps others avoid the same mistakes and identifies patterns across multiple victims.

Working With Legitimate Publishing Professionals

Work with legitimate professionals who provide genuine value for reasonable fees.

Real publishing professionals have a track record you can check. They give you references. They tell you honestly what they can and cannot do.

Professional editors belong to organizations like the Editorial Freelancers Association and can provide samples of their work along with client testimonials.

Legitimate designers maintain portfolios of recent work and can explain their creative process and revision policies clearly.

Real marketing professionals provide clear strategies, measurable goals, and honest assessments of likely outcomes based on your platform and genre.

Good publishing professionals exist. The job is knowing how to tell them from the ones who will take your money and disappear.

Don't let fear of scams prevent you from publishing, but don't let desperation for success make you easy prey for predators. Take time to research, ask questions, and verify claims before spending money on any publishing service.

Your book deserves professional treatment. Take the time to verify anyone you hire before you write a check. The money you spend on a scammer is money you cannot spend on editing, cover design, or anything else that actually helps your book.

Conclusion: Choose Your Path and Get Published

I started this book with the sick feeling I had when I clicked Publish on my first book in 2016 and nothing happened. I want to end it by telling you that the sick feeling never fully goes away, and that's fine.

Every book launch I've done since that first one has carried some version of that anxiety. The difference between then and now isn't that I've become fearless about publishing. It's that I know exactly what I'm doing when I hit the button, which platforms I'm publishing on and why, what my cover is designed to communicate, what keywords I'm targeting and what I expect them to do. The anxiety doesn't go away. The guesswork does.

That's what this book was supposed to give you. Not confidence, confidence is earned through experience. Competence. A clear picture of what each platform actually does, what it costs, and whether it fits your situation.

The Odds, Honestly

Most books don't make money. I'm not going to soften that. The majority of self-published books sell fewer than 100 copies, earn back less than their editing investment, and fade into the catalog inside six months.

The authors who do make money aren't necessarily better writers. They understand the business side. They treat their covers as sales tools, not art projects. They research keywords before they title their books, not after. They publish more than one title. They build email lists before they need them. They pick platforms that fit their genre instead of defaulting to whatever their writing group uses.

None of that is glamorous. It's just the work.

Which Path

If you're still not sure which publishing path fits you, here's the shortest version I can give you.

The short answer: Amazon KDP plus Draft2Digital. Get your book on Amazon and distribute wide through D2D. It costs nothing to set up, your ebook is live in 24-48 hours, and you're in every major market within two weeks. This is the right starting point for almost everyone.

Premium print books, academic works, anything targeting physical bookstores: Add IngramSpark. Get your files right, accept that it takes two months to appear in retail channels. The credibility and distribution access are worth it if your book genuinely competes in that market.

Traditional publishing: If you have a platform, a genuinely commercial book, and the patience to spend two or three years on the submission process, pursue it. If you don't have all three of those things, don't.

Hybrid publishing: Only if you can afford to lose the money entirely and you have a specific reason why self-publishing won't serve your goals. Research the company until you're satisfied, then research them again.

What I'd Tell Myself in 2016

Stop obsessing over platforms and start obsessing over your cover and your title. Those two things determine whether anyone clicks on your book. Everything else, keywords, categories, pricing, and distribution, only matters after someone sees the cover and reads the title.

Hire a copy editor before you publish, not after you get a one-star review about typos. The review stays forever. The typos don't have to.

Publish the second book faster than you think you should. The first book sells better once the second one exists. That's not a theory. It's what happens consistently across genres and platforms.

Don't confuse publishing a book with building a publishing business. Publishing a book takes weeks. Building a business takes years. Both are worth doing, but they're different projects with different timelines and different measures of success.

Go Publish

I've written over a hundred books since 2016. Not all of them are good. Several of them were learning experiences I'd rather forget. But every one of them taught me something I used on the next one, and the cumulative effect of all that publishing is a business that generates real income and sends readers to my ghostwriting practice every month.

You don't need a perfect plan. You need a good-enough plan executed competently and then improved based on what you learn. The authors who are still waiting to get everything right before they publish are still waiting.

You have what you need. Go publish your book.

Appendix: Publishing FAQ

The fifty most common questions authors ask about publishing, answered directly.

This appendix has 139 entries organized into 22 topic sections. You do not read it front to back. Use the section headings to find the topic you need, or search for a keyword in your document reader. The sections cover general publishing questions, ISBNs, Amazon KDP, IngramSpark, Draft2Digital, cover and interior design, pricing and royalties, audiobooks, scams, formatting, business and tax, series and pen names, traditional publishing and agents, rights and contracts, metadata, and platform operations. If you have a specific question, go directly to the relevant section.

General Publishing Questions

1. Do I need a publishing company to publish my book?

No. You publish directly through platforms like KDP and IngramSpark under your own name or an imprint you create. No intermediary is required.

2. How much does it cost to self-publish?

The platforms themselves are free. Your real costs are editing ($500 to $3,000 depending on type), cover design ($200 to $800 for a custom cover), and formatting ($0 if you do it yourself, up to $300 if you hire out). You can publish a book for under $1,000 with smart choices. You can spend much more without improving the result.

3. What do I need to prepare before uploading my manuscript?

A professionally edited manuscript, a correctly sized cover file, interior pages formatted to your trim size, your book metadata (title, description, categories, keywords), and your ISBN. Have all of these ready before you touch any platform.

4. Do I need a literary agent to publish?

No, for self-publishing. Agents are only relevant for traditional publishing with major publishers. Self-publishing is direct: you upload your book, set the price, and distribute it yourself.

5. What is the difference between self-publishing, hybrid publishing, and traditional publishing?

In self-publishing you do everything yourself and keep most royalties. In traditional publishing a publisher pays you an advance and handles production and distribution, but takes most royalties and controls your book. In hybrid publishing you pay a company for services while retaining more control than traditional, but most hybrid companies charge too much and deliver too little. The chapter on each model covers this in detail.

6. How long does it take to publish a book?

On KDP, your ebook can be live within 24 to 48 hours and your print book within 72 hours. IngramSpark takes two to six weeks to appear across all retail channels. Plan your launch timeline around the slowest platform, not the fastest.

7. Can I publish on multiple platforms at the same time?

Yes, with your own ISBN. Buy your ISBN from Bowker, upload to KDP for Amazon, upload to Draft2Digital for wide ebook distribution, and upload to IngramSpark for print distribution to libraries and bookstores. These do not conflict if set up correctly.

8. Do I need an LLC or business entity to publish?

No. Most indie authors publish as sole proprietors with no issues. An LLC adds liability protection and financial separation that makes sense as your revenue grows. Register a DBA before buying your ISBNs if you plan to publish under an imprint name.

9. What is an ISBN and do I need one?

An ISBN (International Standard Book Number) is a unique identifier for your book. Each format requires its own ISBN: ebook, paperback, and hardcover each need a separate number. You technically do not need one for ebook distribution on some platforms, but you need your own for print distribution through IngramSpark and for any bookstore or library distribution.

10. Should I use a free ISBN from KDP or buy my own?

Buy your own from Bowker if you care about professional distribution. A free KDP ISBN lists KDP as the publisher of record in retail databases, which signals to bookstores and librarians that this is a self-published title on Amazon. Your own ISBN lets you name your imprint as publisher. If you only care about Amazon sales, the free ISBN is fine.

11. Can I use the same ISBN on KDP and IngramSpark?

Yes, if you own the ISBN. That is the point of owning it. Do not use a KDP-assigned free ISBN on IngramSpark or any other platform.

12. Who owns the rights to my self-published book?

You do, entirely and permanently. Self-publishing transfers no rights to any platform. KDP, IngramSpark, and Draft2Digital are distribution services, not publishers in the rights sense. You own the copyright from the moment you write the book and retain all rights regardless of where you publish.

13. *What is a publisher imprint and do I need one?*

An imprint is the publishing name that appears on your book instead of your personal name. It makes your book look like it comes from a publishing company rather than an individual. You do not need one, but it gives your catalog a more professional appearance in trade databases and library systems. Register a DBA for your imprint name before buying your ISBNs.

14. *How do I copyright my book?*

Your book is automatically protected by copyright the moment you write it. To register that copyright formally (which you need for maximum legal protection in case of infringement), file online at copyright.gov for $45 to $65 per work. Registration is not required to publish but is worth doing for books you expect to sell at scale.

Amazon KDP

15. *Should I enroll in KDP Select and Kindle Unlimited?*

KDP Select requires 90-day exclusivity with Amazon for your ebook. In exchange you get access to Kindle Unlimited page reads and promotional tools. It is worth it if your genre has strong KU readership (romance, fantasy, thrillers) and you are comfortable being Amazon-only. Skip it if you want wide distribution or your genre reads better outside KU (most nonfiction, literary fiction).

16. *What royalty rate does KDP pay?*

70% on ebooks priced $2.99 to $9.99 in most territories. 35% outside that range or in certain territories. For print books, 60% of list price minus printing costs for books priced at $9.99 and above, 50% below that, as of June 2025.

18. Can Amazon terminate my KDP account? What happens if they do?

Yes. Amazon terminates accounts with little warning and no reliable appeal process. Your books go dark instantly. The best protection is to maintain IngramSpark distribution for all titles so you have active sales channels the moment KDP goes dark, and keep your own copies of all book files, cover files, and metadata.

19. How do I get my print book on Amazon?

Upload directly through KDP Print. Amazon is the only retailer that gives a real advantage to books published directly through KDP rather than coming through IngramSpark. Use KDP for the Amazon listing and IngramSpark for everything else.

20. What is KENP and how does Kindle Unlimited pay?

KENP stands for Kindle Edition Normalized Pages. When a KU subscriber reads your book, you earn per page read rather than per sale. The rate fluctuates monthly based on the KU global fund divided by total pages read across all enrolled books. As of late 2025 it was approximately $0.0045 per page.

IngramSpark

21. Should I use KDP or IngramSpark, or both?

Both. KDP for Amazon, because you earn more per sale and get better Amazon placement. IngramSpark for everything else, because it gives you distribution to bookstores, libraries, and non-Amazon retailers. They serve different purposes and are not alternatives to each other.

22. How do I get my book into bookstores and libraries?

Distribute through IngramSpark with a wholesale discount of at least 40% (55% for serious bookstore consideration) and returns set to no or yes depending on your cash flow tolerance. Get a PCN number from the Library of Congress before publication. Libraries use OverDrive and Hoopla, which IngramSpark feeds. Bookstores order through the Ingram catalog. Being listed does not guarantee being stocked.

23. What discount should I set for bookstores on IngramSpark?

45% is the practical minimum for most retail consideration. 55% matches traditional publisher terms and gives your book a better chance of making it onto shelves. The higher discount reduces your per-sale royalty, so calculate your break-even price before committing.

24. Should I make my book returnable on IngramSpark?

For fiction and most nonfiction targeting general retail, yes if you can absorb the cash flow hit. Returns happen six to eighteen months after sales and can produce negative royalty statements. For specialty books with dedicated audiences, non-returnable works. When in doubt, start non-returnable and change it when you have financial cushion.

25. How long does IngramSpark distribution take?

Two to six weeks to appear across all retail channels after approval. Amazon specifically can take one to two weeks. Build this into your launch timeline.

26. *What file format does IngramSpark require?*

Print-ready PDF for the interior and cover. Minimum 300 DPI for images. CMYK color mode for color books. Correct bleed and margins for your trim size. EPUB for ebook distribution. IngramSpark will reject files that do not meet these specifications.

27. *How do I prepare a PDF from Word for IngramSpark?*

Set your Word page size to your trim size exactly. Set your margins correctly with adequate gutter. Set up page numbers with section breaks so front matter and body number separately. Export using File, Save As, PDF with Standard quality selected and PDF/A unchecked. Read through the exported PDF before uploading.

28. *What is Book Builder and should I use it?*

Book Builder is IngramSpark's upload interface with two paths: supply your own PDF and EPUB, or upload a Word document and let IngramSpark format it. For simple manuscripts without complex layout, the automated path works. For anything with custom formatting, images, or tables, supply your own files. The automated conversion cannot be trusted for books where presentation matters.

Draft2Digital and Wide Distribution

29. *What does going wide mean and is it better than KDP Select?*

Going wide means distributing your ebook to all platforms rather than exclusively with Amazon through KDP Select. Neither is universally better. Wide works for genres with real readership on Apple Books, Kobo, and other platforms. KDP Select works when your genre has strong Kindle Unlimited readership and you want maximum Amazon visibility.

30. *How do I distribute to Apple Books, Kobo, and Barnes and Noble?*

Use Draft2Digital for a single upload that reaches all three plus OverDrive, Scribd, Tolino, and others. Alternatively, publish directly on each platform for access to promotional programs that D2D-distributed books cannot access. Direct accounts require separate uploads but give you more control.

31. *Does Draft2Digital format my book correctly?*

For simple prose, yes. For books with tables, footnotes, complex formatting, or specific typographic design, D2D strips and replaces your formatting with its own templates. Test the output on multiple devices before launch. Upload a pre-built EPUB if your book design matters.

32. *What happens when I switch from KDP Select to wide?*

You must wait out the current 90-day enrollment period before switching. You cannot go wide mid-enrollment without violating KDP Select terms. After the period ends, do not re-enroll, then upload to D2D and other platforms. Expect a few weeks before you are live everywhere.

Cover and Interior Design

33. *How important is the cover and what should it cost?*

The cover is your most important marketing asset. Readers make buy decisions in under a second based on the thumbnail. A bad cover costs you sales no matter how good the book is. Budget $200 to $500 for a professional designer who knows your genre. A cover that does not match genre expectations will fail regardless of quality.

34. What trim size should I use for my print book?

6 by 9 inches is the standard for most nonfiction and many fiction genres. 5.5 by 8.5 is common for fiction paperbacks. 5 by 8 for smaller books. Use a size that is in IngramSpark's standard dropdown rather than a custom size, so your book is compatible with the full distribution network.

35. How do I format the interior of my book?

Use Word with correct styles applied throughout, Atticus for a template-based approach that exports both PDF and EPUB, or Vellum if you are on a Mac and want premium output. For a first book, Atticus is the easiest option that produces professional results without requiring Word expertise.

36. What is bleed and do I need it?

Bleed is the extra image area that extends 0.125 inches beyond the trim line on all sides, preventing white gaps when the printer cuts the pages. Required for covers on all print books. Required for interior pages that have color, images, or design elements running to the page edge. Not required for standard text pages.

Pricing and Royalties

37. How should I price my ebook?

$2.99 to $4.99 for fiction. $4.99 to $9.99 for nonfiction. First books in a series are sometimes priced lower or free to drive readers into the series. Pricing below $2.99 puts you in the 35% royalty tier on Amazon. Pricing above $9.99 does too. The 70% royalty window is $2.99 to $9.99.

38. How should I price my print book?

Calculate your printing cost first using KDP and IngramSpark cost calculators. Your retail price must cover printing costs, your wholesale discount to retailers, and still leave you a real royalty. Most trade paperbacks in the US retail between $14.99 and $19.99. Pricing below $12.99 often leaves pennies per sale after print costs and discounts.

39. What royalty will I actually earn per book sold?

On Amazon ebooks at $4.99 with 70% royalty: roughly $3.49. On a $14.99 print book through KDP with $3.50 printing costs: approximately $5.49. On the same book through IngramSpark with a 55% wholesale discount: significantly less. Run the numbers for your specific price and format using each platform's royalty calculator before you publish.

Audiobooks

42. What is ACX and how does royalty share work?

ACX is Amazon's Audiobook Creation Exchange where you find narrators and distribute to Audible, Amazon, and Apple Books. Royalty share means a narrator produces your book for free in exchange for 50% of royalties for seven years. It eliminates upfront cost but is often more expensive long-term than paying a narrator outright if your book sells consistently.

43. Should I go exclusive with Audible or distribute wide?

ACX exclusivity locks you in for seven years in exchange for 40% royalties. Non-exclusive through ACX pays 25%. Going wide through Voices by INaudio (no exclusivity, 80/20 split) lets you reach Audible, Apple Books, Kobo, Hoopla, OverDrive, and more at the same time. If you already distribute ebooks wide, wide audiobooks are the consistent choice.

44. How much does it cost to produce an audiobook?

Hiring a narrator costs $150 to $400 per finished hour, which works out to roughly $900 to $2,800 for a full novel. The royalty share arrangement costs nothing upfront but gives the narrator 50% of royalties for seven years. AI narration through ElevenLabs runs under $100 for a full novel at current pricing and is appropriate for genre fiction and practical nonfiction, though less so for memoir and literary work where voice carries more of the meaning.

45. Is AI narration acceptable for commercial audiobook release?

Yes, for most genres. The quality of AI narration tools has improved to the point where listeners accept it for genre fiction and practical nonfiction. Audible accepts AI-narrated books with disclosure. The category where it underperforms is memoir and highly personal material where a human voice carries meaning that AI cannot replicate.

Scams and Predatory Publishers

46. How do I tell the difference between a legitimate publisher and a vanity press?

Legitimate publishers pay you. Vanity presses charge you. If you are paying to be published, you are self-publishing through a middleman who takes a cut of your money and sometimes a cut of your royalties. The only thing you should pay for in traditional publishing is your agent's commission after they sell your book. Any upfront fee from a publisher is a red flag.

47. Are hybrid publishers worth it?

Rarely. Legitimate hybrid publishers are selective and reject manuscripts that do not meet their standards. Most companies calling themselves hybrid publishers will publish anything for money. Do the math: if you pay $10,000 and make $5 per book, you need to sell 2,000 copies to break even. Most books do not sell 2,000 copies. Hire freelancers and keep the margin.

48. What red flags should I look for in a publishing contract?

Rights that do not revert when your book stops selling. Option clauses requiring your next book at unfavorable terms. Royalty rates below industry standard (10-15% for traditional). Fees charged to the author for any reason. Vague delivery terms with no enforceable timeline. No audit rights. Any contract where you pay upfront is not a publishing contract.

49. How do I avoid publishing scams?

If it sounds too good to be true, it is. No publisher can guarantee bestseller status or specific sales numbers. Legitimate publishers do not cold-pitch authors. Legitimate agents do not charge reading fees. Anyone asking for money before your book is sold is either a service provider (which is fine, price accordingly) or a scam.

Formatting and Production

51. What font should I use for my book interior?

Serif fonts are standard for print books. Georgia, Garamond, Baskerville, and Palatino are all appropriate. Georgia is widely used and readable at 11 to 12 point. Avoid decorative or sans-serif fonts for body text. Ebook readers override your font choice anyway, so the font decision matters primarily for print.

52. What is a widow or orphan and do I need to fix them?

A widow is a single line from the end of a paragraph sitting alone at the top of a page. An orphan is a single line from the beginning of a paragraph stranded at the bottom of a page. Both look unprofessional in print. Fix them by adjusting line breaks, paragraph spacing, or using Word's widow/orphan control setting. They do not matter in ebooks because text reflows on every device.

53. *What goes in the front matter of a book?*

At minimum: half title page (just the title), full title page (title, subtitle, author, publisher), and copyright page. Optional depending on your book: dedication, table of contents, foreword, preface, introduction. Fiction typically has fewer front matter pages than nonfiction. Your page numbering should start after the front matter, which uses Roman numerals or no numbers.

55. *How do I set up headers and footers in a print book?*

The standard convention is: author name in the header on left-hand (even) pages, book or chapter title on right-hand (odd) pages, with page numbers in the footer or in the header outer corner. Chapter opening pages traditionally have no header. Use Word section breaks to suppress headers on chapter openers and front matter pages. Different sections need different header/footer settings.

56. *What line spacing should I use for my print book interior?*

Most professionally formatted books use 1.2 to 1.5 line spacing for the body text, not the double spacing you use in a manuscript. Double spacing is for editing. Tight single spacing is hard to read. Find a line spacing that gives the text room to breathe without leaving the page looking empty. Your trim size affects this too: a smaller page needs tighter line spacing than a large format.

57. Do I need a table of contents in my book?

Nonfiction always needs a table of contents. Readers move through it looking for specific sections and a TOC is how they get there. Fiction is more flexible, and conventional wisdom says skip it, but a TOC does no harm and helps readers find their way back to favorite chapters. For ebooks, both formats need a clickable linked table of contents, not a list of page numbers. Calibre and Atticus both generate linked ebook TOCs automatically.

58. What is BISAC and do I need to know it?

BISAC (Book Industry Standards and Communications) codes are the standardized category system used by publishers, distributors, libraries, and bookstores. IngramSpark uses BISAC codes for distribution. KDP has its own category system. When you set up a book on IngramSpark, choose the BISAC codes that most accurately describe your book's content and genre. The right codes affect where your book appears in library and bookstore catalogs.

59. Can I update my book after it is published?

Yes, on all platforms. Upload a revised interior file and the new version replaces the old. On KDP, readers who have already purchased can request the updated version. On IngramSpark, revisions are now free as of early 2026. On D2D, upload the new file and it propagates to retailers within a few days. Previously printed copies are not affected, only new orders going forward.

60. What is a proof copy and do I need to order one?

A proof copy is a physical copy of your book ordered before you approve distribution. It lets you see the actual print quality, check that colors look right, verify margins are correct, and catch formatting problems that look fine on screen but are wrong in print. Yes, order one for every print book before you approve distribution. The cost is a few dollars plus shipping. The alternative is discovering a major error after readers have the book.

64. What is the KENP page count and how is it calculated?

Amazon normalizes all KU books to a standard page length before counting pages read. Your actual page count in your book file is not what gets paid. A 300-page book might have a KENP count of 250 or 350 depending on how the text density and formatting interact with Amazon's normalization algorithm. You can see your KENP page count in your KDP dashboard after publishing.

65. Can I change my book's price after publishing?

Yes, at any time on all platforms. KDP price changes take effect quickly. IngramSpark price changes propagate to retailers within a few days to a couple of weeks. D2D price changes vary by retailer. Price changes to your print book do not affect existing inventory at retailers, only new orders.

66. Can I publish a hardcover edition?

Yes. KDP offers a limited hardcover option in casebound format only, available in a handful of trim sizes. IngramSpark offers broader hardcover options including case laminate, jacketed hardcovers, and clothbound. For anything beyond a basic hardcover, IngramSpark is the right platform. Hardcover pricing needs to be higher to absorb the increased printing cost while leaving a real royalty.

67. What is the difference between casebound and jacketed hardcover?

Casebound (case laminate) has the cover design printed directly on the boards, no separate dust jacket. This is cheaper and more durable. Jacketed hardcover has a separate paper dust jacket over plain boards. Traditional publishers use jacketed hardcovers for most trade releases. For indie authors, casebound is more practical and still looks professional. IngramSpark offers both.

68. How do I publish a color interior book?

Color interiors are available on both KDP and IngramSpark but at significantly higher printing costs than black and white. A 200-page full-color book on KDP prints for around $8 to $12, compared to $3 to $4 for black and white. This makes the retail price of color books much higher to maintain any royalty. Set your files to CMYK color mode, not RGB, before uploading. Check IngramSpark's current color printing cost calculator for exact figures.

69. What is the difference between matte and gloss covers?

Matte covers have a flat, non-reflective finish that feels more sophisticated and hides fingerprints. Gloss covers are shiny, make colors pop, and attract attention on a shelf but show every fingerprint and scratch. Genre conventions apply: romance and thrillers typically use gloss, literary fiction and serious nonfiction typically use matte. Soft-touch matte (available through IngramSpark) adds a premium velvety feel at extra cost.

70. How do I publish a children's picture book?

Children's picture books require color interiors and specific trim sizes. KDP supports standard children's book sizes including 8.5 by 8.5 and 8 by 10. IngramSpark has more options including landscape formats. The key difference from text-heavy books: all images must be embedded at 300 DPI minimum, in CMYK mode, and the bleed setup is critical because images often run to the page edges. Budget significantly more for printing costs than a text book.

71. *Do I owe taxes on my book royalties?*

Yes. Royalties are self-employment income in the United States. You owe income tax on net profit and self-employment tax of 15.3% on the first $160,200 (as of 2024) of net self-employment earnings. Keep records of all publishing-related expenses, including editing, cover design, formatting, and platform fees. These are deductible business expenses that reduce your taxable profit.

72. *What publishing expenses are tax-deductible?*

Editing, cover design, formatting, platform fees, proof copies, ISBNs, software subscriptions used for publishing, courses and books about publishing, and a portion of your home office if you use it regularly and exclusively for your writing business. Keep receipts for everything. If publishing is a business rather than a hobby, these expenses offset your royalty income for tax purposes.

73. *How do international royalties work?*

Platforms withhold taxes at different rates for international sales depending on tax treaties between countries. US authors typically have their withholding reduced or eliminated by completing the required tax forms on each platform. International authors may have different withholding rates depending on their country's treaty with the US. Complete the tax interviews on KDP, D2D, and IngramSpark carefully to minimize unnecessary withholding.

74. *How often do the platforms pay royalties?*

KDP pays approximately 60 days after the end of the month in which sales occurred. IngramSpark pays quarterly. Draft2Digital pays monthly for sales from all the platforms it distributes to. ACX pays monthly. Payment thresholds vary: KDP requires a minimum balance before paying, typically $10 to $100 depending on payment method. Set up your payment information correctly before publishing or your royalties sit in limbo.

75. What is the minimum balance required before KDP pays me?

The threshold depends on your payment method and currency. By direct deposit in the US, it is typically $10. By check it is $100. By wire transfer it is $500. Sales that do not reach the threshold in a given month roll over. If your book sells only a few copies, it can take several months to accumulate enough to trigger payment.

Series, Pen Names, and Catalog

76. How do I set up a series correctly on KDP?

Enter the same series name with identical spelling across all books in the series. KDP links books with matching series names and displays them together on Amazon. Inconsistencies, like an extra 'The' or different capitalization, will make Amazon treat them as separate series. Check that all books show the series link after publishing.

78. Can I publish under multiple pen names?

Yes. Most platforms allow multiple pen names under one account. KDP handles this transparently. IngramSpark allows you to publish different imprints and author names through one account. The practical concern is separating audiences: readers of your cozy mystery pen name and your dark thriller pen name are different people and should not be cross-marketed to each other.

79. What happens if I publish a book in a series and then want to change the series name?

On KDP you can update the series name in your book details, but changes propagate slowly and can create inconsistencies during the transition. If your series is still small, change it early and update all books at once. If you have many reviews and established rankings, changing the series name disrupts how Amazon links and presents the books. Think carefully before changing an established series name.

80. Can I publish the same book in multiple languages?

Yes. Each language version should be uploaded as a separate book with its own ISBN, title page in the target language, and category selections appropriate to that market. KDP allows you to upload translated versions and target specific Amazon marketplaces. IngramSpark distributes internationally. If you do not speak the target language, hire a professional translator and have the translation reviewed by a native speaker.

Traditional Publishing and Agents

81. What does a literary agent actually do?

An agent submits your manuscript to publishers, negotiates contract terms, handles rights sales including foreign and film rights, and acts as your advocate with the publisher for the life of the book. They earn 15% commission on domestic sales and typically 20% on foreign rights sales. A good agent has established relationships with editors at relevant publishers. You do not pay an agent until they sell your book.

82. *What is a book proposal and when do I need one?*

A book proposal is a formal pitch document required for nonfiction submissions to traditional publishers. It includes a market analysis, overview of the book, chapter outline, sample chapters, and your author platform information. Fiction writers typically send the completed manuscript rather than a proposal. If you are pursuing traditional publishing for nonfiction, write the proposal before you write the book.

83. *How long does it take to get a traditional publishing deal?*

The realistic timeline runs like this. Finding an agent takes one to six months of querying. Once you have an agent, the submission process to publishers takes one to twelve months. Contract negotiation adds another one to three months. From signing to publication is twelve to twenty-four months. Total from completed manuscript to bookstore: two to four years in a typical scenario. Some books move faster. Many move slower or never sell.

84. *What is a book advance and do I have to pay it back?*

An advance is money paid upfront against future royalties. You do not pay it back in cash if the book fails. However, you earn no royalties until the book has sold enough copies to repay the advance through royalty accrual, a state called earning out. Most traditionally published books never earn out their advance. If you receive a $15,000 advance and the book generates $8,000 in royalties, you keep the advance but receive no additional royalty payments.

85. What happens to my book if my traditional publisher goes out of business?

Your rights should revert to you if the publisher ceases operations, but only if your contract has a proper reversion clause. Without one, the rights may end up with whoever acquires the publisher's assets. This is one reason agents push for clear rights reversion language. If you cannot get royalty statements or payments from your publisher, consult a publishing attorney about options for reclaiming your rights.

Rights, Formats, and Account Operations

86. Can I see who bought my book?

No. Platforms do not share customer data with authors. You see aggregate sales numbers by territory and format but no individual buyer information. This is one of the core arguments for building a direct mailing list: readers who sign up for your newsletter are the only customers you have a direct relationship with. Everyone else belongs to Amazon, Apple, or whatever platform sold the book.

87. What is an EPUB and how is it different from a MOBI file?

EPUB is the standard ebook format used by Apple Books, Kobo, Barnes and Noble, and most other platforms. MOBI was Amazon's internal format for Kindle. Amazon discontinued MOBI for new uploads in 2022 and now uses KFX format internally, though they accept EPUB and convert it themselves. You should distribute your ebook as EPUB. Do not worry about MOBI for any current publishing workflow.

88. What is the difference between ebook exclusivity and print book exclusivity?

KDP Select exclusivity applies only to your ebook. You can publish your print book anywhere while keeping your ebook in KDP Select. Your print book can be on IngramSpark for bookstore distribution while your ebook is exclusive to Amazon. These are entirely separate distribution decisions.

89. What is expanded distribution on KDP and should I use it?

KDP's expanded distribution option attempts to distribute your print book beyond Amazon through Ingram. Do not use it. The discount KDP offers to retailers through expanded distribution is lower than what IngramSpark offers directly, making your book less attractive to bookstores and libraries. Set up IngramSpark separately for non-Amazon print distribution and disable KDP's expanded distribution.

94. What is print run and do I have one as an indie author?

A print run is a quantity of books printed at once. Traditional publishers print in bulk. Indie authors using print-on-demand have no print run. Each copy is printed individually when ordered. This eliminates inventory risk and upfront printing costs, but means your per-unit printing cost is higher than bulk printing. Print-on-demand is the right choice for almost all indie authors unless you have a specific reason to need bulk stock.

96. What is a large print edition and should I publish one?

A large print edition is formatted at 16 to 18 point font instead of the standard 11 to 12 point, for readers with visual impairments. Atticus has a large print export option. It is a separate ISBN and a separate listing on retail platforms. For nonfiction with older audiences or any book where accessibility matters, a large print edition can reach readers who cannot use the standard edition. The market is real but small.

97. What is the difference between self-publishing and vanity publishing?

In self-publishing you upload your files to platforms like KDP or IngramSpark, pay nothing upfront, and earn royalties directly from sales. In vanity publishing (including most hybrid publishers) you pay a company to publish your book for you. The finished product may look similar but the economics are opposite. Self-publishing costs nothing to list; you pay for services like editing and cover design separately and directly. Vanity publishing bundles those services with an upfront fee and typically takes a percentage of royalties on top.

98. Do I need a barcode on my print book cover?

KDP and IngramSpark add the barcode automatically when they generate your print files. You do not need to include it in your cover design. If you are designing the cover yourself, leave a white space in the lower right corner of the back cover where the barcode will be placed. Some cover designers include a placeholder; others leave it blank and trust the printer to add it. Either approach works.

99. What does it mean when Amazon shows my book as unavailable or out of stock?

For print-on-demand books, this should not happen under normal circumstances since books are printed as ordered. If it does, it usually indicates an issue with your KDP account, a content review being triggered, or a metadata mismatch. Log into your KDP dashboard to check for alerts. For IngramSpark books appearing on Amazon through Ingram, out-of-stock messages sometimes appear during Ingram catalog updates and usually resolve within a few days.

100. *What is a Library of Congress Control Number (LCCN) and do I need one?*

An LCCN is how the US library system catalogs books. It goes on your copyright page and in your IngramSpark metadata. Libraries use it to catalog acquisitions. Getting one is free and takes about a week through the Preassigned Control Number (PCN) program at loc.gov/publish/pcn. You need your own Bowker ISBN (not a KDP-assigned one) and a publishing imprint to be eligible. Submit before your publication date since the number must be assigned before the book is printed.

Cover Production Details

101. *What goes on the spine of a print book?*

The title, the author name, and optionally your publisher imprint logo. The title should be the most prominent element. Text on the spine reads top to bottom in most English-language books. Spine width is calculated by IngramSpark and KDP based on page count and paper type. Use their calculators before designing. A spine that is too narrow for the text you want to fit looks amateur and is sometimes rejected.

102. *What goes on the back cover of a print book?*

The book description, any endorsement quotes, your author bio (brief), the barcode with ISBN, and your publisher imprint information. The description and endorsements are the selling elements and should dominate the space. The barcode goes in the lower right corner. Do not crowd the back cover. White space reads as professional. Bookstores and librarians scan back covers to evaluate stock decisions.

103. *Can I design my own book cover?*

Yes, and many authors do. The risk is that cover design has genre conventions that are not obvious to non-designers. A cover that looks attractive to you may signal the wrong genre to readers or look amateur at thumbnail size. If you design your own cover, study the top fifty bestselling covers in your specific category before starting, test your design at 100 pixels wide, and get honest feedback from other authors in your genre rather than friends and family.

104. What image rights do I need for my cover?

You need a commercial license for any image used on a book cover sold for money. Stock photo sites like Adobe Stock, Shutterstock, and Depositphotos sell commercial licenses. Free image sites like Unsplash offer licenses that sometimes permit commercial use and sometimes do not. Read the specific license for each image before using it. AI-generated images have unresolved copyright status; check each platform's current licensing terms. Never use an image you found on Google without verifying the license.

105. What resolution do cover images need to be?

A minimum of 300 DPI at the final print size. A cover designed at 72 DPI (screen resolution) will look pixelated and blurry in print. Design at full size in the correct dimensions at 300 DPI from the start, not at a small size that you scale up. For ebook covers, a minimum of 2,500 pixels on the longest side is standard, with 1,600 by 2,560 pixels being the KDP recommended size.

106. What is a dust jacket and do I need one?

A dust jacket is a separate paper cover wrapped around a hardcover book's boards. Traditional publishers use them for most trade hardcovers. Indie authors can order jacketed hardcovers through IngramSpark. They are not required. Casebound hardcovers with the design printed directly on the boards are more practical, more durable, and cheaper. Jacketed hardcovers make sense for books targeting traditional retail where the format signals premium positioning.

107. What file format should I submit for my cover?

A high-resolution PDF with bleed marks and crop marks, in CMYK color mode, at 300 DPI. IngramSpark and KDP both accept this format. RGB images will be converted by the printer with unpredictable color shifts. Provide your cover designer with the exact spine width from the platform's calculator before they finalize the file. A cover submitted with the wrong spine width will be rejected.

Editing

108. What is developmental editing and when do I need it?

Developmental editing addresses the structure of your book: plot, pacing, character, argument flow, chapter organization, and whether the content actually works. It happens before copy editing, often before the book is finished. You need it if your manuscript has structural problems, if you are a first-time author working in a new genre, or if early readers are telling you something is off but they cannot say what. It is the most expensive type of editing and the most valuable for books with fundamental problems.

109. What is line editing and how is it different from copy editing?

Line editing works at the sentence and paragraph level, improving clarity, rhythm, and style. Copy editing works at the grammar, spelling, punctuation, and consistency level. Line editing makes the prose better; copy editing makes it correct. Many editors do both in one pass. If you hire an editor, confirm which services are included so you know what you are getting.

110. *How do I find a reputable editor?*

Ask for referrals from authors in your genre whose books you consider well-edited. Check the Editorial Freelancers Association directory. Look at editors who specialize in your genre and ask to see their client list and testimonials. Request a sample edit of the first ten pages before committing. Any editor worth hiring will offer a sample. Be wary of editors who cannot show you published books they have worked on.

111. *How do I know if my manuscript is ready for editing?*

You have revised it as much as you can on your own. You have read it aloud and fixed the obvious problems. You have had at least one beta reader give you feedback and you have addressed their concerns. You are not paying an editor to fix problems you know about and can fix yourself. The cleaner the manuscript you send to an editor, the more their attention goes to real problems rather than surface issues.

112. *Should I hire a proofreader separately from a copy editor?*

Yes, for any book going to print. A copy editor fixes errors in the manuscript. A proofreader checks the formatted file, the actual PDF or EPUB that will be published, for errors introduced during the formatting process. These are different tasks at different stages. A book that was clean after copy editing can have new errors after formatting: lines that break wrong, footnotes that move, text that reflows. The proofreader is your final quality check before publishing.

113. What is the KDP dashboard and what can I track there?

The KDP dashboard shows units sold, page reads (for KU books), royalties earned by title and territory, and advertising spend if you run Amazon ads. It does not show you individual buyer information. Reports are available by day, month, and custom date ranges. The KENP report shows page reads separately from sales. Download monthly reports and keep your own records. KDP's dashboard does not maintain historical data indefinitely.

114. What is KDP's AI content disclosure requirement?

Amazon requires authors to disclose whether their book contains AI-generated content, defined as content created by AI even if subsequently edited by a human. AI-assisted content, where AI helped with grammar or suggestions but a human wrote the text, does not require disclosure. The disclosure is made during the upload process and does not appear publicly on the book page, but providing false information violates KDP's terms. When in doubt, disclose.

115. What happens if KDP rejects my book?

KDP sends an email explaining the reason for rejection. Common reasons: cover or interior files do not meet technical specifications, content violates content guidelines, metadata contains prohibited terms, or the book is a duplicate of an existing listing. Fix the specific issue identified and resubmit. If the rejection reason is unclear, contact KDP support for clarification before resubmitting.

116. Can I publish a book on KDP that I also sell on my own website?

Yes, for print books. KDP print exclusivity does not exist. You can sell print books directly from your website while having the same book available on KDP. For ebooks, KDP Select exclusivity means you cannot sell the ebook elsewhere during enrollment. If you are not in KDP Select, you can sell your ebook on your own site and on KDP at the same time.

117. What is the KDP Pricing Support tool?

A feature in KDP that suggests a price for your book based on comparable titles and conversion data. The suggestion is algorithmic and not always appropriate for your book. Use it as a data point, not a directive. Knowing your genre's pricing conventions and your own break-even costs is more useful than following an algorithm's suggestion.

118. Can I publish a book that was previously self-published elsewhere on KDP?

Yes. Prior self-publication elsewhere does not disqualify a book from KDP. The exception is KDP Select: if you want to enroll in KDP Select, your ebook must not be available for sale or free download anywhere else, including your own website, other retailers, or any other platform.

119. How do I set up an IngramSpark account?

Go to ingramspark.com and create a publisher account. You will need your business name or imprint name, tax information, banking details for royalty payments, and your ISBN prefix if you have one. IngramSpark charges no setup fee. Before uploading your first book, download IngramSpark's file creation guide for your trim size to ensure your files meet their specifications.

120. What is IngramSpark's eProof process?

After uploading your files, IngramSpark generates a digital proof that you review before approving distribution. This is not a physical copy. it is a PDF rendering of how your book will print. Check every page for layout errors, text that runs into margins, and image quality. Once you approve the eProof, IngramSpark begins distribution. If you need changes after approval, revisions are now free as of early 2026.

121. How does IngramSpark handle international distribution?

IngramSpark has print facilities in the US, UK, and Australia, and distribution partnerships in Germany, Italy, Poland, India, Japan, China, Brazil, South Korea, and Singapore through their Global Connect program. Your book becomes available to wholesalers and retailers in those markets after distribution approval. International sales appear in your IngramSpark dashboard with royalties paid in your currency after conversion.

122. Can IngramSpark distribute my ebook to Amazon?

Yes, but do not enable this option if you are also publishing directly on KDP. Running both creates duplicate listings, pricing conflicts, and catalog confusion. Use KDP for your Amazon ebook listing and disable Amazon distribution in IngramSpark. Use IngramSpark's ebook distribution for all other retailers.

123. What is IngramSpark's market access fee?

IngramSpark charges 1.875% of the net revenue from each sale as a market access fee, in addition to printing costs for print books. This is built into their royalty calculation and is not a separate charge you pay directly. For most books, it is a small amount per sale. It is worth knowing it exists so your royalty calculations reflect the actual take-home amount.

124. What platforms does Draft2Digital NOT distribute to?

Amazon. D2D does not distribute to Amazon for ebooks or print. Use KDP directly for Amazon. D2D also has a prohibited content list that includes certain categories of books. Self-publishing guides are one example, excluded due to market saturation from AI-generated content. Check D2D's current prohibited content list before uploading any book in a potentially restricted category, as prohibited titles can have their accounts locked.

125. Does Draft2Digital offer print distribution?

Yes, through a partnership with IngramSpark's network. The practical issue is that print through D2D gives you less control than going directly to IngramSpark, and the discount and terms passed to retailers may differ from what you would set directly. For serious print distribution, set up IngramSpark directly. D2D print is adequate for authors who want simplified distribution and are not targeting physical bookstores.

126. What is D2D's royalty rate?

D2D takes 10% of the list price as their fee, with the remainder going to you after the retailer's share. On Apple Books where the retailer takes 30%, D2D takes 10%, leaving you with 60%. The exact amount depends on each retailer's terms. D2D provides a royalty estimator in their dashboard.

Note that as of May 2026, D2D charges a $12 annual maintenance fee per account for accounts earning under $100 net per year across all their titles combined. It is not charged per book. If your total D2D earnings exceed $100 net per year, the fee does not apply.

127. *Can I use D2D and publish directly on Apple Books or Kobo at the same time?*

Yes. D2D's distribution is non-exclusive. You can distribute through D2D and also have a direct account on Apple Books and Kobo. The practical issue is pricing consistency: if you set different prices through each channel, readers may find your book at different prices on the same platform depending on which listing they find. Keep prices consistent and disable D2D distribution to any platform where you have a direct account.

Lulu and Audiobook Platforms

128. *What is the difference between Lulu Direct and Lulu Global Distribution?*

Lulu Direct sells your book only through Lulu.com at the highest royalty rate, around 80% of profit margin. Global Distribution sends your book to Amazon, Barnes and Noble, and major retailers through Ingram's network at a lower royalty. Extended Distribution adds bookstore and library ordering through Ingram's full wholesale network. Each tier reaches more buyers but returns less per sale.

129. *When does Lulu make sense over IngramSpark?*

When print quality is the primary concern and your book benefits from better paper, binding, or color printing than KDP Print provides. Cookbooks, art books, photography collections, and technical manuals with many images are the best candidates. For simple text-heavy books, IngramSpark's quality is adequate and its distribution is more direct.

130. What audio file specifications does ACX require?

MP3 files at 192 kbps or higher, constant bit rate. Each chapter must be a separate file. Files must include room tone at the beginning and end of each recording. The finished audio must have no background noise, consistent volume, and pass ACX's quality check tool before submission. Recordings that fail quality check are rejected and must be resubmitted.

131. What is Findaway Voices and is it still operating?

Findaway Voices rebranded as Voices by INaudio in August 2025. It is the same service under a new name: a wide audiobook distribution aggregator that places your audiobook on Audible, Apple Books, Kobo, Hoopla, OverDrive, and dozens of other platforms with no exclusivity requirement. The 80/20 royalty split in the author's favor and the lack of exclusivity are the core advantages over ACX exclusive.

132. How do I find a narrator for my audiobook?

ACX has a narrator marketplace where you post your project and narrators audition. You can also post on Voices123 or Voice123 and receive auditions from professional voice actors. For royalty share arrangements, ACX is the standard platform. For paid narration, you can hire directly from ACX, through narrator marketplaces, or by contacting narrators whose work you have heard and admire. Always request an audition of your specific material before hiring.

133. What is ACX quality check and how does it work?

ACX runs an automated quality analysis on uploaded audio files that checks for peak levels, noise floor, and room tone compliance. Files that fail are flagged with specific errors. ACX also provides a quality check tool you can download and run on your files before submission, which prevents rejection. Run the tool locally before uploading to catch problems early.

134. What are subsidiary rights and should I retain them?

Subsidiary rights are the rights to exploit your book beyond the original publication: translation rights, film and TV adaptation rights, audiobook rights, serialization rights, merchandise rights, and more. In traditional publishing contracts, publishers often claim some or all of these. In self-publishing you retain all of them automatically. If you sign any contract that grants subsidiary rights, understand exactly what you are giving away and for how long.

135. What is a rights reversion clause in a traditional publishing contract?

A rights reversion clause defines the conditions under which your rights return to you if the publisher fails to perform. The trigger is typically the book going out of print or falling below a minimum sales threshold. Traditional contracts used to define out of print as no physical copies available. Now publishers argue ebooks keep books technically in print indefinitely. Negotiate for a specific sales threshold: if the book earns below a defined amount in a defined period, rights revert to you.

136. Can I republish a book I originally published with a traditional publisher?

Only if your rights have reverted or you have terminated the contract. Review your contract for the reversion clause. If rights have not reverted, contact your agent or the publisher's rights department to request reversion. If the book is still generating any royalties, reversion is harder to obtain. If the publisher has been acquired or gone out of business, the rights situation can be complex and may require legal counsel.

137. What is a work for hire and how does it affect ownership?

In a work-for-hire arrangement, you write content and the person or company paying you owns the copyright. Ghostwriting is typically work for hire. The client owns the book and the copyright; you receive payment but have no ongoing claim to royalties or ownership. If you are ghostwriting, clarify ownership terms in your contract before you start writing.

138. What is creative commons licensing and can I use it for my book?

Creative Commons licenses allow you to specify how others may use your work: whether they can share it, adapt it, use it commercially, and under what conditions. Some authors license nonfiction under Creative Commons to encourage wider distribution while retaining commercial rights. For most commercial fiction and nonfiction, standard copyright with all rights reserved is the appropriate choice. Creative Commons is a publishing decision, not a legal requirement.

Industry Terms and Production Process

139. What is typesetting and is it different from formatting?

Typesetting and formatting are often used interchangeably for book production. Technically, typesetting refers to the professional process of arranging text and visual elements on the page, originally done with physical type. In modern indie publishing, it means the same as interior formatting: setting fonts, spacing, margins, headers, and chapter breaks so the book looks professional. A typesetter is a formatter; the terms mean the same thing in this context.

140. What is a galley or ARC and how is it different from the final book?

A galley (also called an advance reading copy or ARC) is an uncorrected pre-publication version of the book. Traditionally these were physical copies with a disclaimer on the cover noting they were uncorrected proofs. Indie authors typically produce digital ARCs through BookFunnel. The key difference from the final book: errors may still be present, and the book may change before publication. ARCs sent to reviewers should include a note that the text is not final.

141. What is a colophon and do I need one?

A colophon is a brief statement at the end of a book describing production details: the typefaces used, the paper, the printer, sometimes the edition. Traditional publishers include them in some books, particularly literary fiction and specialty editions. Most indie authors do not include one. It is optional and serves readers who care about book design and production details.

142. What is a Library of Congress Cataloging in Publication (CIP) data block?

CIP data is the cataloging information that appears on the copyright page of traditionally published books, assigned by the Library of Congress to help libraries catalog acquisitions. It is only available to traditional publishers and hybrid publishers with established relationships with the Library of Congress. Indie authors cannot get CIP data. The PCN (Preassigned Control Number) program is the available alternative, which gives you an LCCN for your copyright page without the full CIP block.

143. *What is an edition and when should I publish a new one?*

An edition is a version of a book that contains substantive changes from the previous version. A new edition gets a new ISBN. For nonfiction: publish a new edition when the content has changed enough that earlier readers would benefit from the updated version, or when significant factual information is outdated. For fiction: new editions are rare and usually reserved for significant revisions. An updated cover or corrected typos is not a new edition. It is a revised printing of the same edition.

144. *What is print quality inspection and should I order more than one proof?*

Print-on-demand quality can vary slightly between print runs and between different printing facilities. For a new book, order one proof from KDP and one from IngramSpark if you plan to use both. Compare them. Check for consistent color, paper weight, cover lamination quality, and binding. If you are producing a color book or a premium product, order multiple proofs to check consistency. Save one proof copy as a reference standard for future comparison.

Metadata and Distribution

145. *What is THEMA and how does it differ from BISAC?*

THEMA is an international book subject classification system used in European markets and increasingly globally. BISAC is the US standard. IngramSpark asks for BISAC codes for US distribution. Some international distribution systems use THEMA. For most indie authors publishing in English for US and UK markets, BISAC is the relevant system. If you are targeting European markets specifically, understanding THEMA codes can improve your book's discoverability in those catalogs.

146. What is the difference between list price and net price?

List price is what a consumer pays at retail. Net price is what IngramSpark or the retailer reports to you as the basis for your royalty calculation, after the retailer's discount has been subtracted. If your list price is $15.99 and the retailer takes a 55% discount, the net price is $7.20, and your royalty is calculated as a percentage of that. Always calculate your expected royalty from the net price, not the list price.

147. What is metadata and why does it matter for distribution?

Metadata is all the descriptive information about your book: title, subtitle, author name, ISBN, description, categories, keywords, publication date, page count, price, and format. Every retailer and library system uses metadata to catalog and display your book. Inaccurate or incomplete metadata causes your book to be miscategorized, makes it harder for readers to find, and can cause catalog rejections. Get it right before you publish and keep it consistent across all platforms.

148. What is an ONIX feed and do I need to know about it?

ONIX (ONline Information eXchange) is the standard format publishers use to transmit book metadata to retailers, distributors, and library systems. IngramSpark generates and sends ONIX feeds on your behalf when you enable distribution. You do not need to create or manage ONIX feeds yourself. Knowing it exists helps you understand why metadata changes on IngramSpark take time to propagate. The ONIX feed goes out on a schedule, not instantly.

149. What is an ARC tour and how does it work for publishing?

An ARC tour is a coordinated distribution of advance reader copies to a group of reviewers who agree to post their reviews around the publication date. Indie authors typically run ARC tours through services like BookSirens, NetGalley, or BookFunnel, or by managing their own ARC reader list. The goal is to have reviews ready at launch rather than starting from zero. An ARC tour is a publishing logistics task; the reviews themselves are a marketing outcome.

150. What is a book's pub date and does it matter?

The publication date is the official date your book is available for sale. On KDP it is the date you publish. On IngramSpark you set it when uploading, and distribution starts from that date. The pub date matters for library and bookstore ordering, for establishing which award eligibility periods your book falls into, and for any pre-launch advance review copies. Setting an IngramSpark pub date at least six weeks out gives you time for distribution to establish before you promote the book.

151. What is a press kit and what goes in it for a published book?

A press kit (or media kit) contains the materials a journalist, blogger, podcast host, or event organizer needs to write about or interview you: your author bio in short and long versions, a high-resolution author photo, the book cover image at 300 DPI, the book description, key talking points or themes, and your contact information. It is a publishing infrastructure document, not a marketing campaign. Having one ready before publication means you can respond to any media inquiry immediately.

152. What is self-publishing versus indie publishing and is there a difference?

The terms are used interchangeably by most people in the industry. Some authors prefer indie publishing because it positions the work alongside indie music and indie film rather than associating it with vanity or failure. Others use self-publishing as the accurate technical term. The distinction matters only in perception, not in any practical publishing process. What you call it does not change how platforms, distributors, retailers, or readers treat your book.

153. What is the difference between a publisher and a distributor?

A publisher is responsible for producing the book: editing, design, formatting, and bringing it to market. A distributor places the finished book in retail and library channels. Traditional publishers often handle both functions. For indie authors, you are the publisher and platforms like KDP, IngramSpark, and D2D are your distributors. Ingram is specifically a distributor: it does not publish books, it places books that others have published into its wholesale network.

About the Author

Richard Lowe is a professional ghostwriter and publishing consultant who has published over 100 volumes across multiple platforms since 2016. His clients include Fortune 500 executives, New York Times bestselling authors, and industry leaders seeking to establish thought leadership through professional publication.

As a former IBM Senior Technical Staff Member and IT consultant with over 30 years of experience, Richard brings analytical precision to the often confusing world of publishing platforms and strategies. He has personally navigated every major publishing option covered in this guide, from Amazon KDP exclusivity through wide distribution and professional print networks.

Richard's ghostwriting clients regularly face publishing decisions, leading him to develop clear, unbiased frameworks for platform selection based on actual business goals rather than marketing promises. This book consolidates years of real-world experience helping authors make informed publishing choices.

His work spans business books, memoirs, technical guides, and fiction across genres. Richard currently publishes through Amazon KDP, Draft2Digital, IngramSpark, and other platforms, giving him ongoing insight into platform changes and optimization strategies.

Richard operates The Writing King, providing ghostwriting and publishing consultation services to clients worldwide. He resides in Clearwater, Florida.

Books by Richard Lowe

See books by Richard Lowe at
https://masterofworlds.com

Get free publishing insights and industry updates at
https://thewritingking.substack.com

For ghostwriting and book coaching services see
https://thewritingking.com